Leaders with Substance

An Antidote to Leadership Genericism in Schools

Matthew Evans

First Published 2019

by John Catt Educational Ltd,
15 Riduna Park, Station Road,
Melton, Woodbridge IP12 1QT

Tel: +44 (0) 1394 389850
Email: enquiries@johncatt.com
Website: www.johncatt.com

ISBN: 978 1 912906 57 4

Set and designed by John Catt Educational Limited

This book is dedicated to Eleanor and Beth. Simply awesome.

Praise for Leaders with Substance

'Is leadership even a thing?' From the get-go, *Leaders with Substance* packs the punches. Champions of the 'charismatic hero leader' you've been warned, for this is not simply 'another book about leadership'. This is a book that systematically pulls apart the ill-defined and abstract theoretical field of leadership, reconstructing it with pragmatic, expertise-fuelled substance about what leaders need to know to effectively perform their duties. For you don't have to look too far for pontification about leadership with many ideas and beliefs shared from personal insight and experience. However, whilst personal anecdotes are both rousing and inspiring, they rarely offer a concrete framework for leaders to refer to in real time and in increasingly challenging contexts.

Leaders with Substance skilfully makes the case for the importance of building bodies of knowledge to develop leadership expertise that will, in turn, enable us to solve problems in our own contexts and the specific tasks we are faced with. It directly challenges deeply-held beliefs about what a successful leader looks like and how best to 'replicate' this. And like all good sources of professional learning, it prompts an 'intentional interruption', challenging us to distil our concept of leadership without reverting to generic and ambiguous words and phrases that have typically galvanised the leadership discourse. This is a book that has extracted the superfluous anecdotal rhetoric and injected substance into the concept of school leadership. A must-read for anyone intent on honing their leadership expertise.

Kathryn Morgan, Associate Dean, Learning Design (Leadership Programmes), Ambition School Leadership

Just as pedagogy in schools has often lost its object – the thing being taught – so, Matthew Evans argues, has leadership. Far from being a generic skill, leadership requires extensive domain-specific knowledge. This book, like Matthew's blog, had me gripped. It rang true on every page as an honest and probing account of what so easily goes wrong, at school and system level. The substance of the goals we pursue really matter. The detail of how those goals are secured, especially the eternal renewal of curriculum quality and teacher knowledge, matters fundamentally. Our analytic focus needs to be on such matters of substance, both in executing and in analysing leadership.

Christine Counsell, Independent Education Consultant and Trustee, David Ross Education Trust

This is, quite simply, the book I wish I had read ten years ago. It dissects the concept of leadership expertise through a complex and original blend of research, philosophy and cognitive science. Even Obi-Wan Kenobi can illuminate the persistent problems of school leadership. Intelligently written, it examines different perspectives, offers a wide-ranging research base, and never dictates. It is far more than a manual or guide, for it eloquently invites you to think about the 'swampy' problems inherent in the complexity of school leadership. Offering both solace and humour in a frank and eminently readable style, it cuts to the heart of the issues with concision. Whether you are sunburnt by the early experiences of leadership or weathered by its seasons, Matthew offers an intelligent analysis and exploration of the landscape and ways to navigate it without losing your moral compass. A thoroughly enjoyable and thought-provoking read which changes the narrative on school leadership.

Emma White, Assistant Headteacher, Farmor's School, Gloucestershire

Matthew writes with a rare humility, especially rare in books about educational leadership. Instead of stating a claim and seeking to convince you of its truth, Matthew tentatively opens a debate and asks you to join him on a trek across the mountains and swamps of school leadership. Punctuated with personal experiences, vignettes and analogies, *Leaders With Substance*, contests the notion of leadership as it is usually understood, and instead asks us to consider the domain-specific knowledge required to avoid genericism and 'management flannel'.

With a curious combination of self-depreciation and quiet confidence, Matthew's writing presents complex intellectual arguments alongside practical strategies that leaders can apply immediately. From a series of questions on disciplinary knowledge to eleven Spinal Tap-style vignettes for a reconstructed view of leadership, this book is one of the most useful books on leadership I have encountered. And yet it also a deeply reflective book, almost philosophical in its unrelenting questioning of deep-seated beliefs about leadership.

One of the most challenging books on leadership I have ever read, *Leaders with Substance* requires immediate re-reading. I want to reconcile the seeming contradiction between a rejection of situational leadership alongside support for the fluid execution of domain-specific knowledge in different contexts – aren't they the same thing? At times the arguments seem semantic; are we relegating leadership to a euphemism because it doesn't meet the conditions of scientifically testable concept whilst also advocating it as an expression of integrity, empathy, purpose and service to our community – which are also scientifically untestable concepts? This is what I love most about *Leaders with Substance* – the challenge, the invitation to join Matthew on a mountain trek where walking the terrain and veering into parts marked 'unexplored' on the map.

I want to explore the terror of unconscious incompetence and make sure I'm not suffering from a 'God complex', but I'm not ready to abandon my faith in my personal charisma. This is what Matthew's book does to you – it startles you, then recalibrates you. You may not agree with everything Matthew writes, but he doesn't ask you to. Instead, he asks you to question what tangible benefits a concept of leadership brings us and challenges you to defend your personal perception of it. Whilst I struggle to accept I've been duped by a leadership fallacy all these years, I do see that asking what is the 'stuff' of leadership is infinitely more useful than reading books full of 'executives pontificating'.

In *Leaders with Substance*, Matthew presents a refreshing, reconfigured view of leadership which is grounded in domain-specific knowledge. At times I foolishly thought Matthew had veered off topic, he'd accidentally been diverted towards the realms of curriculum, knowledge, cognitive science, intelligence and accountability – and then the penny dropped. This is the substance of leadership.

This is a book on leadership which is completely devoid of arrogance. It is also a book full of heart, driven by integrity and propelled by purpose. I can't wait to read it again.

Carly Waterman, Headteacher, Lodge Park Academy, Corby

Headteacher Matthew Evans has written a fascinating book that is perfectly attuned to his distinctive voice, full of refreshing honesty and authority. Evans' writing is well known for its intellectual depth, curiosity and even its devilishly playful questioning of the accepted facts. His book explores the substance of leadership in this contrary, restless and provocative style. Each chapter looks at leadership from a school context and undoes as many myths as it provides platforms to build ideas upon. Evans' engaging style uses many interesting cultural tidbits and knowledge that help to explain the main subject of the book: military theorists, presidential history, research on intelligence, string theory and current Ofsted debate all get discussed and challenged in terms of what leadership is and if it actually exists.

This is an excellent book on leadership and worth reading. It is not a simple airport bookshop guide to being the sharpest saw, or the organisational architect. Instead it is a book for edu-grown ups; a witty, smart and credible discussion of a very stretchy concept.

Jude Hunton, Vice Principal, Nicholas Chamberlaine School, Warwickshire.

In this book Evans writes about education leadership in a unique way. He suggests there is no grand theory of leadership; certainly not one that could be summed up in a textbook. He critiques 'transformational approaches' and the charismatic leader beloved of the Blairite years. Instead he posits a slower, more organic and sustainable route to school improvement and leadership that is rooted in domain knowledge and school context, creating cultures that are pupils and staff oriented rather than shaped around the pursuit of data.

Evans understands the need for an enriching curriculum and asks leaders to be understanding of the core purpose of a school – to teach the curriculum really well – and is rightly sceptical of the myriad of vision statements that seem vacuous, stating aims that seem to be far removed from the classroom. He argues, instead, for a moral compass and ethical approach that guide leaders in their work.

This is the noble work of a contrarian, who sees leadership as part and parcel of a school's culture and not something learnt generically away from being in a school.

Highly recommended.

Martin Robinson, education consultant and author

Contents

Foreword by Jen Barker and Tom Rees...13

Introduction...15

Section 1: The Dominance of Leadership Genericism in Schools......23

Chapter 1: Is leadership even 'a thing'? 25

Chapter 2: Hollow skills...35

Chapter 3: Do we need clever leaders?...47

Chapter 4: Model leadership 61

Chapter 5: Transient turnarounds..73

Chapter 6: Abstraction and distraction...83

Chapter 7: Curricular genericism 95

Chapter 8: Leaving genericism behind 107

Section 2: The Substance of Leadership 115

Chapter 9: Expert leaders..117

Chapter 10: What makes school leadership unique?..........................133

Chapter 11: Portraying purpose..147

Chapter 12: Empathy..159

Chapter 13: Scripts..169

Chapter 14: Indicators of change 179

Chapter 15: Leadership in its place...193

Section 3: Substantially Better Leadership 201

Chapter 16: Our leadership inheritance 203

Chapter 17: A leadership curriculum and pedagogy 211

Chapter 18: Failure to learn 225

Chapter 19: Leadership knowledge 233

Chapter 20: A new leadership orthodoxy 243

Acknowledgements 249

Foreword

by Jen Barker and Tom Rees

Leaders with Substance is a refreshing and important addition to the literature on school leadership. In writing it, Matthew presses the reset button on the leadership orthodoxy, stops some of the common narratives in their tracks and asks us to consider the work of school leaders through a different lens.

We know the difference that leaders can make to a school is significant, yet their work is complex and the conditions in which they operate can be enormously challenging. Moreover, research within the leadership field offers little by way of a definitive solution to these challenges. *Leaders with Substance* is honest about this problem and addresses it head on.

In this book, Matthew provides a detailed account of the challenges faced by school leaders and explores a range of factors that have contributed to them. His work is very clearly underpinned by a deep appreciation of school context and a desire to improve the experience of everyone involved in schools. The result is impressive: a careful interrogation of the term leadership, a lens through which the work of leaders may be more carefully examined, a rejection of the genericism that has dogged leadership for so long and a credible alternative to extant theory.

For those of us who work in education, reading this book provides plenty to think about. It will challenge readers' thinking – sometimes to the point of discomfort – but always for the better. It will leave them more knowledgeable, sceptical of prevailing orthodoxies and equipped with a new language for leadership. *Leaders with Substance* is an important contribution to the literature on leadership, one that anyone involved in school leadership should read.

Jen Barker is Dean of Ambition Institute and Tom Rees is Executive Director of Ambition Institute and author of Wholesome Leadership: the Heart, Head, Hands and Health of School Leaders.

Introduction

What do I know about leadership?

This book has been over 30 years in the making. I've thought about leadership a lot during this time. I've also been a leader in schools, in one capacity or another, for two decades; so I've put what I've learnt into practice, too. And yet I still have a strong sense of imposter syndrome. Who am I to write a book about leadership? What could I possibly have to say?

As a youthful academic failure, one of the only things I salvaged from my schooling was an A Level in business studies. I hadn't intended to take it; it was one of the only subjects the college would let me do with my mediocre grades at O Level. Nonetheless, I was taken with the subject – by which I mean I found it interesting, not that I did any work for it. I remember learning about motivation: Maslow's Hierarchy of Needs, Taylorism and the Hawthorne experiments.[1]

I was intrigued by organisational structures, quality assurance and even accountancy. This was real, concrete; in marked contrast to the equations I struggled to understand in maths.

Armed with my A Level (singular), I faced the prospect of starting up a sandwich shop; my dad's attempt to salvage me from unemployment, as no university would have me. Fortunately, a career serving wraps to commuters passed me by as I scraped into a Higher National Diploma in Business and Finance. Suddenly I was in the heart of London, studying alongside other academic rejects. This was the era of Saatchi and Saatchi

(Margaret Thatcher's advertising agency of choice); of big spending on corporate PR; of giant brands and a booming financial sector. Capitalism was in the ascendency and business leaders were high profile and highly paid. A future in marketing lay ahead.

Or so I thought. Instead, the economy dived and the dole queue beckoned. After nine months, I begged my way into a shop assistant job in an off-licence. A year later, bored, frustrated and wondering what to do with my life, I decided to become a teacher... of business studies, obviously. I somehow convinced the University of Brighton to allow me on to a two-year BA degree, with Qualified Teacher Status.

For the first time, I studied and I worked. Teaching the topics I had found so engaging to other people was deeply gratifying. I stayed one step ahead of the A Level students; learning the material the night before enabled me to bluff my way through their lessons. On to my first job in a deprived coastal town and, after only a year, my first post of responsibility, covering the careers co-ordinator on maternity leave. I became interested in organisational culture and management theory, reading the likes of Charles Handy[2, 3, 4] and Tom Peters.[5, 6] I learnt about behavioural norms, situational leadership, group dynamics and management by objectives. I watched the leaders of the schools in which I worked, critiquing their leadership style, beginning to think to myself, 'I could do that'. At last, an opportunity to cut my teeth as a head of department – theory into practice – and teaching A Level economics for the first time, filling the shoes of my predecessor, who happened to be an Oxford economics graduate, making a promise to my headteacher that I would not, in her words, 'f**k up' the economics results.

Exorcising the ghosts of the past, I signed up with the Open University for an MA in education management to prove to myself that I wasn't the academic dunce that my CV suggested. More leadership theory; this time intermingled with curriculum, assessment and pedagogy.

And on... assistant head in charge of the school's business and enterprise specialism; then deputy head, with the terrifying prospect of writing my first timetable. Having exhausted the management literature, my attention turned to economics, politics and philosophy: anything with a 'big idea' that could help me understand the world better.

Finally, headship: the ultimate testing ground for nearly 30 years of reading about, studying, thinking and practising leadership.

Six years into this challenge, I can confidently say that everything I've learnt about leading schools has proven invaluable, but that nothing could ever have fully prepared me for being the person with whom the buck stops. Suddenly you are expected to know everything but feel like you know almost nothing. What could that lazy, mediocre student possibly know about running a school?

My career looks, in retrospect, like climbing a promotional ladder, but it has never been about anything as crass as ambition. It has always been about a fascination with organisations: how you shape them and how they shape you. And about getting bored really easily. What is amazing to me is that, despite everything I've read and experienced, I'm still not sure what leadership actually is. I'm not sure anyone else is, either.

Time to write

I really don't have the time to write a book. Being a headteacher keeps you fairly busy. I am also conscious that I'm putting my neck on the line in daring to write a book about leadership. I am not the perfect leader, and in some people's eyes, I will fall far short of even being a competent one. In my defence, this isn't a book that claims to teach you how to be a great leader. I'll address what this book does claim to do in a moment. Firstly, I need to explain what drives me to write this.

I have a deep sense of disquiet about some of the nonsense I see going on in schools in the UK. There are many brilliant schools and dedicated people out there, and I have rarely met anyone working in a school whose motives I doubt. But somehow things have become warped across the system. It appears to me that leaders in some schools have lost sight of what schools are there for and, frankly, they are making some pretty stupid decisions. I don't think they are entirely to blame for this. There are forces at work, which bend their behaviour and distort priorities. To compound the problem, the professional development we provide for our school leaders doesn't cut the mustard in an era when the challenges schools face seem greater than ever. We (as an educational system) need to get a grip.

Many of the mistakes I've seen have also been mistakes I've made myself. It is embarrassing to think about some of the drivel I've come out with over the years and some of the initiatives I've launched on an unsuspecting staff. I've always had an affinity with the teacher-curmudgeon who sits in the sagging chair in the staffroom and criticises everything school leaders try to implement. Their cynicism strikes a chord with me and I like to think that if I had a longer attention span and could have stuck at one job for more than a few years, I might have ended up as one of them. My regret is that I didn't listen to them more when they told me that what I was about to do wouldn't work. They were often right. I'd like to channel their voice a little in this book; not in their relentless negativity but by imagining their response to the claims I will make. They can smell bullshit a mile away.

My main motivation, however, is that I have rediscovered the joy of writing, thanks to a community of teachers and school leaders on social media, many of whom are bloggers and authors themselves. The democratisation of authorship that the internet has facilitated has given many practitioners a voice, and this collective voice is beginning to change public policy. At its best, this movement draws on a base of research and evidence that, it seems to me, is leading to an era of rationality and enlightenment in educational discourse in the UK.

This book, therefore, is an attempt to set out what I think we need to do as school leaders to get things back on track in our schools. It is born of frustration, mishaps and hope.

What has substance got to do with this?

This is not a handbook. It is not full of practical ideas. It will also not present a grand theory of leadership, or models and frameworks, which you often find in management literature. There are plenty of books out there that do these things, but this is not one of them.

Rather, this book will present a way of looking at what school leaders do: a perspective. It isn't the only valid way to consider leadership, but I believe it offers a different perspective to that presented in much of the literature. I hope it will help you to see the work of school leaders in a new way and, in doing so, lead to some fresh thinking about this important topic.

I would like you to imagine that reading this book is like putting on a pair of glasses. These are special glasses as they bring into focus the 'substance' of school leadership. They have a built-in filter, which means we will no longer see the things we don't need to see. What will these lenses filter out?

- **Abstract theories:** The field of leadership is full of models and grand theories about what leaders are and do. They help us to organise our knowledge about leadership, but they can also divert attention from the concrete reality of the work at hand. We should try to look past theory and focus on the specifics of the job of improving schools.

- **Distractions:** The UK education system is like a mischievous demon, distracting us from the task of running schools for the benefit of the children within them with initiatives, targets and political whims. Our goal, as leaders, is to keep our eyes on the school and learn to ignore the noise around us.

- **Ideology:** Rather than be drawn into philosophical debates, we should look for evidence of what works in our schools.

- **Management flannel:** The educationalist Christine Counsell once said of something I wrote, that it was 'utterly devoid of management flannel'.[7] I took it as a compliment. My wife put it more plainly when she asked if this book would be called 'Leadership without the bullshit'. If we cut through the bluster, avoid the jargon and set aside our egos, perhaps we'll discover that leadership is actually quite straightforward.

When all the above is filtered out, what I hope we will see is the *substance* of leadership, by which I mean:

Substance: the matter of which the thing consists.

What do leaders actually need to know?

How is this knowledge developed into expertise?

Substance: the most important or essential part of something.

Where should school leaders focus their attention?

What will make the most difference to the children in our schools?

Substance: a meaningful and valid point ('the argument has substance').

What do we know to be true about leadership?

What evidence do we have to support our claims?

The structure of the book

Applying the glasses analogy further, the book is structured in the following way:

Section 1: The Dominance of Leadership Genericism in Schools

What is it we are trying to see through?

Section 2: The Substance of Leadership

Putting the glasses on to begin to see the substance of what leaders know and do.

Section 3: Substantially Better Leadership

How we might develop leaders, and schools, with substance.

Chapter summaries

The concept of substance is also used to summarise each chapter according to what we need to know, why this knowledge is important and how we know it to be true. In doing so, I intend to make a series of substantiated claims which, when taken together, form an overall picture of leadership from this perspective.

Style over substance

The tone of each chapter may vary a little, and even the style of writing within a chapter. While I want to base this book on evidence, I do not want it to be a dry, academic text. I am a practitioner, not an academic (therefore please forgive any sloppiness regarding referencing – I'll do my best). However, I do not want to write a book of anecdotes. To make this book readable and justifiable, I may jump between evidence and example. I may also fail to delve deeply into the research which underpins the more academic sections of the book; again, for the sake of brevity and readability. For those wishing to know the detail, I will reference research and suggest further reading where appropriate. As a new author, I am still finding my 'voice', so if anything doesn't flow or read well, it is my fault and no one else's.

So, let's begin. I hope that, by the end, we will both understand leadership a little bit better.

References

1. Pick up any A Level business studies textbook – the same old theory is still being taught.

2. Handy, C. (1991) *The Age of Unreason.* Brighton, MA: Harvard Business Review Press.

3. Handy, C. (1997) *The Hungry Spirit.* New York, NY: Broadway Books.

4. Handy, C. (2015) *The Second Curve.* London: Random House.

5. Peters, T. and Waterman, R. H. (1982) *In Search of Excellence.* London: Profile Books.

6. Peters, T. (1994) *The Pursuit of Wow!* London: Pan Books.

7. Christine Counsell is an author, academic and curriculum developer. Her blog can be found here at www.thedignityofthethingblog.wordpress.com

Section 1

The Dominance of Leadership Genericism in Schools

Chapter 1
Is leadership even 'a thing'?

I will make an assertion which might undermine the existence of this book: leadership may be neither a satisfactory nor useful concept. Despite the millions of words written on the subject, I'm not sure it even is a subject. I question whether there is such a thing as leadership at all. This, therefore, is a book undergoing an existential crisis. If this book were a teenager, it would be growing its hair long and playing acoustic guitar. It would be staring up at the night sky and asking, 'What are we actually here for?' What is the purpose of a book about leadership which questions whether the term has any definable boundaries or utility?

It is the quantity of literature on the 'subject' of leadership that adds weight to my doubts. Among the realms of conjecture, supposition and speculation on the meaning and substance of the term, it appears to me that no consistent definition has emerged, no cogent theoretical framework, no coherent construct that has any reliable, predictive powers. One might go so far as to say that 'we seem to remain intent on calling almost everything leadership'.[1]

Reaching for a definition

What exactly do we mean when we talk of leadership? It is sometimes used as a collective term, scooping up a range of personality traits, behaviours, attitudes or characteristics. Such attempts to capture commonalities in what effective leaders *are*, try to distil leadership down to its essence, to find out what is left when the superfluous is boiled away. One such model I came across in researching this book is the 'Fundamental 4 Competencies for Leaders' proposed by the Center for Creative Leadership;[2] these are, apparently, self-awareness, communication, influence and something called learning agility. Now, few people would argue with the importance of being a good communicator, and it would be difficult to imagine anyone leading anything without communication of some sort. We could probably find a range of research studies to evidence how effective communication helps organisations achieve their goals. So we can claim that competency in communication is important – possibly fundamental. It is questionable, however, whether you could define *self-awareness* as a competence, where competence means something you can *do* successfully. Self-awareness may be thought of as having a conscious knowledge of one's own character and feelings; it is something we possess more than something we can perform.

The third fundamental competence, influence, may more correctly be considered something you can be more or less successful at, but the concept is so broad as to be almost meaningless. Should we take this to mean persuasion (like a salesman), coercion (like a dictator) or subconscious influence (like a con artist)? And is influence truly a personal characteristic, or a function of position and access to power? As for the fourth fundamental competence, learning agility, well... let's not even go there.

The above example illustrates the difficulties in trying to categorise and distil what it is *to be* a successful leader. The things we are grouping together are rarely conceptually consistent, the selections made are often arbitrary and the items selected are broad and ill-defined.

Leadership is also sometimes defined as a *style* or *approach*. Rather than what competencies the leader possesses, these models describe the ways the leader might proceed. For example, we know leaders make decisions, but how are these decisions made? Is the leader consultative (listening and responding to the views of others) or autocratic and commanding? Some such theories attribute leadership style to personality types, while others advocate the adoption of different approaches to suit the context within which one leads; the art being in varying one's style to suit the situation.

When we talk of leadership in this way, do we simply mean 'this is how I prefer to get things done' or 'I vary my approach as I need to'?

We do not seem to be able to settle on a theory of leadership, or to agree what the boundaries of a theoretical framework might be. Indeed, Bass (1990) argued that 'there are almost as many different definitions of leadership as there are persons who have attempted to define the concept'.[3]

Ephemeral leadership

To understand why leadership appears so difficult to pin down, we can turn to the work of a military officer teaching managerial studies at the US Air Force Academy: Lieutenant Colonel Yoos. In 1984, Yoos published a paper entitled, 'There is no such thing as leadership!'.[4]

Yoos' paper set out 'not to debunk leadership per se, but to show that clinging tenaciously to the euphemism leadership is counterproductive to the vital pragmatic task of understanding and regulating human behaviour'. Yoos argued that leadership fails to meet the conditions of a scientifically testable construct; firstly because there is no agreed definition for the term, and without this there is no basis for research into whether it explains or predicts social phenomena. Furthermore, Yoos questioned whether the term has any substance or meaning which adds value to other concepts already defined: 'What knowledge would be foregone, what insight lost, if the term "leadership" were expunged?', he asks.

Yoos' challenge to us is to establish an agreed definition and 'theory' of leadership which adds something to our knowledge of how organisations work. If we are unable to meet this challenge, then what purpose does discussion of leadership serve?

The human resource

Being in charge of an organisation or function within an organisation means directing resources towards the achievement of organisational goals. What does the term 'leadership' add to our understanding of this process? This question is often phrased as 'what is the difference between management and leadership?'. The answer often given is 'people'.

People are a resource, but most of us find it a distasteful way to consider human beings and acknowledge that 'directing' people is an unsatisfactory way of describing the complex process of ensuring that the attention of 'the people' (our employees or team) is focused on achieving a shared goal. We don't just place human resources in the right location, configure them correctly and maintain them so that they don't break down. We prefer the term 'leadership': the acceptable face of management which acknowledges the complexity of the human condition and the need to 'influence' (as the Center for Creative Leadership points out) rather than direct. Seen in this way, we may define leadership as 'behaviour, in a group context, that results in the willing compliance of the members'.[5]

But what behaviour will result in willing compliance? For there to be a robust theoretical framework for leadership, we need to be able to identify these behaviours, develop a model that will explain what we see happening in organisations and predict the impact of a leader's actions. The difficulty is that the efficacy of various behaviours will be dependent on situational factors; the same behaviours may not work equally well in different contexts. All situations in which we may identify the need for leadership are different, in terms of the technical dimensions of the task (what the task entails), the social context (who is involved), and the organisational context (cultural, structural and political factors). The behaviours required of the leader will necessarily vary in relation to the specific circumstances. And so we arrive at the loose field of 'situational leadership'.[5]

Situational leadership is an attractive concept, but to what extent can we claim it is a theory of leadership? Imagine we ask the question, 'what makes a great leader?' (a reasonable question to which a robust theory of leadership should be able to provide an answer). If the answer is that it depends on what situation the leader is in, then the theoretical construct is not about the leader and their qualities, but instead about the social dynamics, psychology and capabilities of the group. Situational leadership is a theory of group behaviour, not of leadership. A true theory of leadership would be able to identify the consistent qualities possessed by the 'great leader': qualities which cut across time, place and context. Situational leadership theory does not overcome Yoos' challenge, in that the term 'leadership' adds nothing to our understanding of group dynamics; the utility in the theory is in the word 'situational', not 'leadership'. If the word was 'expunged' and replaced with another, what would we lose? 'Situational management' or 'group effectiveness theory' would serve equally well. In this theory, at least, the concept of leadership appears ephemeral, ungrounded and without substance.

In the end, Yoos asked, Is (sic) it advantageous to pretend that there is a thing called leadership? In answering his own question, No! He (sic) mentioned literature that is full of artefact and generalizations, executives pontificating but only reciting stories about their experiences, and, worst of all, promising to students the 'holy grail' and delivering nothing but confusion and frustration. His answer to these questions – would not a rigorous study of social psychology serve better?[6]

Leadership genericism

What if we were able to identify a set of behaviours which, through rigorous research, could be proven to be associated with successful leaders? How might we go about this, and what benefits would this knowledge bring?

These behaviours are correlated with their success, perhaps even shown to be causal in some way. An example of this is research carried out by Ashkenas and Manville for the *Harvard Business Review*, and published as the HBR Leaders Handbook.[7] The authors conclude that the 'best leaders... almost always deploy these six classic, fundamental practices:

1. Uniting people around an exciting, aspirational vision.

2. Building a strategy for achieving the vision by making choices about what to do and what not to do.

3. Attracting and developing the best possible talent to implement the strategy.

4. Relentlessly focusing on results in the context of the strategy.

5. Creating ongoing innovation that will help reinvent the vision and strategy.

6. "Leading yourself": Knowing and growing yourself so that you can most effectively lead others and carry out these practices.'[8]

To establish the above list, the authors interviewed 'over 40 successful leaders' and reviewed 'several decades' worth of articles from the Harvard Business Review to understand the 'recurring messages from academics and practitioners about what leaders should do'. This approach exemplifies many of the problems with the field of leadership research and theorising. Aside from the question of how a 'successful leader' is defined, there is a heavy reliance on self-reporting by leaders as to what they attribute their success. Furthermore, the authors rely on a literature review of articles which includes both opinion pieces and more evidenced summaries of academic research. What weight should be given to the 'recurring messages' in a theory of leadership? Just because people keep saying something is important, doesn't make it so. Finally, we have no null hypothesis: what research have the authors undertaken into the behaviours of unsuccessful leaders? Might we not find that some or all of the 'fundamental practices' identified are also features of those leaders who fail?

The usefulness of the 'fundamental practices' listed is also questionable. Consider point 1: 'uniting people around an exciting, aspirational vision'. We may find that most, or even all, successful leaders oversee teams or organisations that subscribe wholeheartedly to a common 'mission' and work relentlessly towards shared goals as a consequence. However, might this be a consequence of the context of the organisation rather than a special ability of the leader? We might imagine that uniting people in the just cause of reducing homelessness might be somewhat more achievable than inspiring them to supply the best drain covers money can buy. No doubt the book sets out how leaders have set about communicating an exciting, aspirational vision (at $50, I'm not likely to find out if they have), and there will be case studies of successful leaders to exemplify how this has been achieved (in Yoos' words, lots of 'executives pontificating'), but as CEO of Drain Solutions, what am I to take from this?

When I read such lists, I can't help thinking 'What specifically should I do *right now*, in *my context*, to overcome the *actual challenges* I am facing?' What tangible benefit does the concept of leadership actually bring?

Substance

Leadership theory creates a fallacy when it attempts to describe the traits, characteristics or behaviours of a successful leader. It dupes us into thinking that the secret to success is in developing these aspects in ourselves. Such a quest is foolhardy and without meaning. There is no substance in this pursuit.

'Substance' is a useful term in this debate. It has the power to ground us in pursuing worthwhile activity as leaders. Substance has a variety of meanings, each of which are relevant here. Substance refers to the 'body' or 'material' of something. It leads us to question what it is we are actually talking about – what is the *stuff* of leadership? Substance is tangible, not ephemeral, and we should concern ourselves only with the concrete question of what leadership can deliver. The word also infers importance and significance. If we are to answer Yoos' question about what the concept of leadership actually adds to our understanding of things, we must establish what leadership offers of significance; we have no time for the peripheral. Lastly, substance can be used to imply a meaningful and valid point is being made (often in the negative, as in 'the argument lacks substance'). Our case for the importance of leadership must stack up.

If we are to rescue leadership from the grasp of genericism and ambiguity, we must give it substance.

Domain expertise

An expert is a person who is an authority in a particular area or topic. For example, an accountant is an authority in accountancy, a lawyer in law, a doctor in medicine. Each field contains more specialist areas: management accountancy, employment law, heart surgery and so on. Experts are defined by a domain of knowledge in which they have gained mastery. Without specialisation and domain-specific knowledge, we cannot have experts.

What might we mean when we talk about an expert leader? To abstract the concept of leadership from a domain of knowledge would leave it floating like a helium-filled balloon. To what is it tethered?

Your answer may be that the expert leader has mastered the art of making decisions, solving problems or motivating employees. But, I ask, what is the nature of those decisions? What specific problems were solved, and what did the leader draw upon to achieve this? What understanding of human nature, or the specific needs and desires of those led, enabled the leader to energise others towards the desired objective? Our expert leader must have mastered a domain of specialist knowledge – what is the substance of this domain?

To talk generically about leadership, as if it is a discipline separate from a domain of knowledge, leaves us only with hollow concepts of skills (see Chapter 2). Leadership with substance (stuff) is rooted in specific knowledge, but what knowledge?

To define a domain of knowledge, we must be more specific about what is being led. Let's start with school leadership. This gives us a context: a narrower field of expertise. Within this, we can identify areas in which school leaders may specialise: curriculum leadership, pastoral leadership, special educational needs. As we zoom in on the functional area within the school context, the domain of knowledge comes increasingly into focus, and the generic leadership traits blur into the background. In this way, we become expert leaders, not in the mystic art of leadership but in the concrete reality of the tasks at hand. We are learning to lead in our specific context, not to generally become great 'leaders of men' (in Woodrow Wilson's words) – or women, for that matter!

What remains of leadership?

'We have been told, again and again and again, that better organisational performance requires better leadership.'[9] Does it?

Washbush calls for substance when he states, 'We need to ask fundamental questions about what will help members of organisations, particularly those in power and authority positions, contribute to better organisational performance.' In doing so, he appears to dispense with leadership, calling it 'a confusing, multi-nuanced witches' brew of inconsistent, often contradictory and confusing propositions'. Ouch! It is indeed unclear as to whether a focus on disciplinary substance leaves any intellectual space for leadership. Is leadership nothing more than the ability to draw upon true disciplinary fields such as philosophy, economics, political science, history, and social psychology, as Washbush claims?

I'm not sure whether leadership is a distinct or useful concept, but I am not ready to throw out the term yet. If nothing else, it serves as useful shorthand for the thing that people do when they want to achieve something meaningful and worthwhile. Things need to be done, and there is an art in moving others towards a purpose. Leadership may be a vague, collective term for a multitude of behaviours, the effectiveness of which may vary wildly from one context to the next, but it does, at least, capture a desire to make a difference, and it acknowledges that the people we manage have value beyond being a 'human resource'.

However, if we are to maintain the pretence of a field of expertise called 'leadership', we must ensure that our consideration of this topic has substance. To my mind, we can ensure this by starting with the domain of knowledge which is required for leaders to practise. This domain includes technical, social and cultural understanding. As school leaders, we lead *this* school, not *any* school. If leadership is to emerge as a robust construct, like the phoenix from the ashes, it will be from the substance of our daily endeavours and not the abstract models of leadership gurus.

Where does that leave this book?

Having questioned the field of leadership as a worthy topic of study (thereby alienating most of the people who might even consider reading this text), where does that leave a book which has the word 'leaders' in its title?

My concern is with the domain of knowledge upon which school leaders draw, and how, when we start by considering the specific job(s) that school leaders do, it changes how we lead. I hope that this is the antithesis to most management books. By starting with the specifics of the matter at hand, and not the theoretical leadership construct, I aim to provide a perspective on leadership which avoids flim-flam, grand theories and untestable ideologies. And in its place, substance.

Summary of chapter substance

▬▬▬▬▬▬ **Substance (stuff)** What do we need to know?	Leadership is an ill-defined theoretical field which often fails to offer useful insights into the specific tasks that leaders are faced with. An abstract notion of leadership, separate from the technical, social and cultural knowledge required in an organisation, adds little to our understanding of what successful leaders do. To rescue leadership as a worthy topic of study, we should consider the substance of what leaders need to know to effectively perform their duties.
▬▬▬▬▬ **Substance (significance)** Why is this important?	Considerable time and energy is spent celebrating, growing and developing better leaders, but to what avail? The effectiveness of schools is too important to be left to rely upon half-formed theories, untestable notions and grand ideas.
▬▬▬▬▬ **Substance (validity)** How do we know it to be true?	Despite decades of theorising and research, no consistent definition of leadership has emerged, and no robust theoretical framework which is scientifically testable.

References

1. Washbush, J. B. (2005) 'There is no such thing as leadership, revisited', *Management Decision* 43 (7/8) pp. 1078-1085.

2. Center for Creative Leadership (2018) 'The Core Leadership Skills You Need in Every Role', *CCI* [Online]. Retrieved from: www.bit.ly/2JopgLZ

3. Bass, B. M. (1990) *Bass & Stogdill's Handbook of Leadership: Theory, Research, and Management Applications* (third edition). New York, NY: The Free Press.

4. Yoos, C. J. II (1984) 'There Is No Such Thing as Leadership, Proceedings of the Ninth Symposium: Psychology in the Department of Defense', *Management Decision* 43 (7/8) pp. 343-347.

5. Hersey, P. and Blanchard, K. H. (1993) *Management of Organizational Behavior: Utilizing Human Resources*, (sixth edition). Englewood Cliffs, NJ: Prentice-Hall.

6. Ibid (n 4)

7. Ashkenas, R. and Manville, B. (2018) The Fundamentals of Leadership Still Haven't Changed, *Harvard Business Review* [Online], 27 November. Retrieved from: www.bit. ly/2AQeV9x

8. Ibid.

9. Zaccaro, S. J. (2007) 'Trait-based perspectives of leadership', *American Psychologist* 62 (1) pp. 6-16.

Chapter 2

Hollow skills

The skill of leading complexity

One of the least pleasant tasks I have had to oversee as a headteacher is redundancy. No leadership books, courses or seminars prepare you for looking someone in the eye and telling them that there is no longer a job for them. Unfortunately, I found myself in this position in four of the first five years of headship.

I will try to avoid being a pontificating executive (Yoos' criticism in Chapter 1) by claiming that I have some wisdom to share about how to manage redundancy well. Instead, I will draw upon this experience to make a point, which is that you don't really have much idea how to do a difficult task until you're doing it, or even until it's all over.

Any complex management problem requires considerable skill to navigate. These skills have names like 'problem solving', 'decision making' and 'communication', and the process of redundancy requires these skills in abundance. One round of redundancies I faced required that I reduce the teaching workforce in my school by 10%. The first issue to consider was how to continue to run a functioning school with such a depleted workforce: what curriculum cuts will be made, which jobs will no longer get done and how will other people's jobs change as a result? Once I identified the required 'surplus', decisions had to be made about which jobs were under threat. The ramifications of these decisions were anticipated and measures taken to mitigate, as far as possible, the collateral damage which would inevitably result.

When faced with complex problems such as redundancy, the decisions take place inside your head, but the process plays out in the real world. How the changes are communicated will be critical to your success. Leaders will deliver staff briefings, one-to-one meetings, formal and informal documentation; each of which adopts the right style, a clear message and is delivered with sensitivity and tact. We cannot doubt that the leader will need to act skilfully to take a school through such a process.

But where does this skill come from? Is it something that the leader *brings* to the task, or does the fluid execution of the task originate in its very substance?

To find the source of the river, consider what the leader needs to know. In the case of redundancy, the knowledge required is extensive and diverse. Firstly, there is a technical domain of knowledge around employment law and due process. For the school leader approaching redundancy for the first time, they are unlikely to already possess this knowledge. Why would they? This is 'need to know' information which will be rapidly acquired through reading and good advice from experts in this area. Then there is organisation-specific knowledge. This includes knowing team structures (so that the 'pool' of those subject to the redundancy process is identified fairly and correctly), roles and responsibilities (to identify which posts are indispensable to the school, for example), information around length of service (important in avoiding unaffordable redundancy costs) and the detail of individuals' qualifications and expertise, often gained through a skills audit (upon which an objective assessment of redundancy can be made). Lastly, the leader requires a rich knowledge of the social bonds and culture of the organisation. Where do allegiances lie, what bonds of friendship may affect the emotional response to redundancy decisions, what collective understanding and misconceptions exist about the redundancy process, who will staff 'blame' for these cuts and what organisational resilience exists? While technical knowledge will help determine what should happen, knowledge of social and cultural aspects will help inform the 'how'.

Consider a newly appointed headteacher (with no prior experience of redundancy) finding themselves in the position of having to cut jobs. They will not reach into their toolbox of leadership skills to tackle this mammoth task. Instead, if they are wise, they will rapidly begin learning what they need to know. To begin making decisions without first equipping yourself with the information you need will simply lead to bad decisions. Good decision making is predicated on understanding the dynamics of the situation within which the decision is to be made; to solve the problem, the problem must be understood. To find a solution, one must be able to anticipate how various options are likely to play out. These are not hollow skills. The fluid execution of the task is dependent on a deep knowledge of the domain: the technical, social and cultural knowledge which relates to the task in hand.

Even communication skills, often cited to be domain-independent (i.e. something you are either generally 'good at' or 'bad at', regardless of context), are almost entirely dependent on contextual knowledge. While we may bring the general ability of being able to speak in sentences to an audience, watch the speaker crumble when they know nothing of substance. Eloquence in public address requires a sophisticated mental model upon which related ideas are ordered and connected. Persuasion is only possible if the speaker understands the desires and motivations of his audience. Confidence is not innate but rather it comes and goes with one's grasp of the topic.

None of this is to say that the skills of problem solving, decision making and communication don't exist, just that they cannot be entirely abstracted from the relevant, contextual domain of knowledge. Leaders don't *bring* skills to the task, they develop fluid execution through repeated application of domain-specific knowledge. As the headteacher gains experience in the redundancy process, they will become (hopefully) more skilled. However, they are not becoming better decision makers, problem solvers or communicators; they are becoming better at making redundancy decisions, solving similar problems and communicating to others the difficult topic of job losses. This betterment is a result of deeper knowledge of the domain and procedural fluidity acquired through repeated practice.

What evidence is there to support the concept of domain-specific skills?

In arriving at the position set out above, I am drawing heavily on the field of cognitive psychology and what sense it has helped me make of my own leadership experiences. The evidence is brought together well in a paper by Tricot and Sweller (2014) titled, 'Domain-Specific Knowledge and Why Teaching Generic Skills Does Not Work'.[1] The paper sets out the case against the historical emphasis on generic skills, arguing instead in favour of domain-specific knowledge. The field of cognitive science is central to many of the arguments I will make in this book, and it is worth setting out some of the claims made in this paper in a little more detail.

Tricot and Sweller use the following definitions in relation to knowledge and skills:

Generic or domain-general skills are those which 'can be used to solve any problem in any area. For example, learning to solve problems by thinking of similar problems with known solutions is an example of domain-general knowledge that can be applied to all problems'.

Domain-specific knowledge is 'memorised information that can lead to action permitting specified task completion over indefinite periods of time'.

The authors' claim is that, as far as we can establish, domain-general skills are biologically primary knowledge,[2] i.e. knowledge which our brains have evolved to acquire naturally. Examples of such biologically primary knowledge (relevant to the topic of leadership in particular) are learning to listen, engage in social relations or learning to use a problem-solving strategy such as a means-end analysis.[3] While, Tricot and Sweller argue, biologically primary knowledge will be learned automatically 'simply as a consequence of membership of a normal society', individuals can continue to learn to apply the skill in a new domain. Where this happens, it is an example of the acquisition of domain-specific rather than domain general knowledge.[4]

Domain-specific knowledge is classed as biologically secondary knowledge, i.e. knowledge which is deemed to be culturally important but that our brains have not yet evolved to acquire automatically.

Tricot and Sweller (2014) review the evidence which supports the assertion that 'learned skill, especially problem-solving skill, derives from acquired domain-specific, rather than domain-general, knowledge'. This evidence comes from studies in areas as diverse as chess, mathematics, music, art, schooling, intelligence, memory, air traffic control, electronic engineering and programming.

Perhaps the most relevant and interesting evidence base for our purposes is the field of 'expertise' research. Research in this area seeks to compare novices and experts within various fields to ascertain what distinguishes the two, and how individuals develop expertise. Experts develop competence in solving complex problems by drawing on domain-specific knowledge, such as the example of redundancy outlined above. Some studies suggest that competence in solving such problems requires knowledge of typical 'problem states' associated with the domain, along with knowledge of how best one might proceed. Tricot and Sweller (2014) state that 'For complex, extensive areas (domain) knowledge may consist of tens of thousands of problem states (Simon & Gilmartin, 1973).[5] Those innumerable problem states and the best moves associated with those states are stored in long-term memory. It is that knowledge that constitutes expertise'.

Tricot and Sweller do not deny the existence of generic skills. However, for generic skills to become useful in tasks that require biologically secondary knowledge (i.e. most imaginable scenarios in which school leaders will find themselves), individuals must learn to apply the skill in a new domain, thereby creating domain-specific knowledge. What determines task-performance is not the inherent quality of the generic skill but the extent and accessibility of relevant domain-specific knowledge held in long-term memory. My use of the 'toolbox' analogy above is intended not to deny the existence of generic skills which can be drawn upon, but instead to highlight the importance of domain-specific knowledge as the first thing to 'reach for'. Once you know what you are dealing with, the biologically-primary toolkit will come in handy but, at the risk of stretching the metaphor, you won't know which tools to use, or how they can help, until you've assessed the task in hand.

If I've managed to convince you that skills cannot be considered as an abstract concept and developed as a general ability, separate from context, then you will join me in disregarding the notion of generic leadership competencies. Competency is the idea that leaders possess generic skills which are transferable and independent of the domain of knowledge. Once attained, these competencies are carried with the leader from one highly paid executive post to the next. In reality, successful leaders have a rich, deep and interconnected body of knowledge relevant to the field in which they lead. This web of knowledge is known as a schema, and it is the source of the leadership Nile.

Leadership schemas

Knowledge and skill are often seen as different things; however, they are two sides of the same coin. We can know something which is explainable (declarative knowledge) or know how to do something (procedural knowledge). Procedural knowledge will lead to effective performance of a task to the extent that it has been practised. For example, in theory, I know how to change a spark plug as my granddad was a mechanic and taught me. However, that was 30 years ago and I am not sure that this knowledge is still sufficiently secure, or relevant to the mechanics of today's cars, in order for me to actually change a spark plug anymore. To strengthen this knowledge, and to develop a secure skill, I would need to practise the procedure of changing a spark plug again and again, preferably with lots of different models of cars. When this skill becomes second-nature, I will be able to carry out the task without much or any conscious thought: it will become automated.

Understanding knowledge and skills is complicated by considerations of the links between the mind and body. For example, when we learn to ride a bike, it is mostly a subconscious process as our body and brain interact to establish balance through minute muscle movements. Declarative knowledge plays little, if any, role in this process. I might encourage my daughter to have a go, console her when she falls off and give 'Dad tips' along the way ('brake!!!'), but most of the learning is happening without my help. We can't teach someone to ride a bike: they just need to keep having a go. There are some such examples in the repertoire of leaders: for example, the ability to speak slowly and clearly, pausing for breath and enunciating well when speaking in public. However, most skills carried out by leaders are more like changing a spark plug than riding a bike, in that they begin with the conscious possession of declarative knowledge (knowing that) and procedural knowledge (knowing how).

A good analogy for leadership knowledge is found in the learning of a foreign language. David Didau (2018), in a blog titled *How to explain... a schema*,[6] uses Mandarin as an example of how a learner becomes fluent in speaking a language. Didau begins with simple vocabulary, connecting the words *ni hao* and *hello* in the mind of the learner as meaning the same thing. This connection can be strengthened through practice; you say ni hao, I say hello. As vocabulary builds, the connection of the Mandarin word to the English 'equivalent' acts as a memory prompt or cue. These prompts may also include images (for nouns), grammatical rules and groups of words. Didau represents this schema as a growing network of interconnected items of knowledge. Clusters of knowledge can then be drawn in to working memory and employed with increasing fluency, until 'you arrive at a point where it becomes automatic and effortless to recall most of the items within a schema and the whole network is thoroughly embedded with other, connected schemas', i.e. you are a fluent speaker of Mandarin.

In conclusion, Didau states, 'This is what it means to be fluent at anything: our ability to draw vast schemas into working memory effortlessly and automatically means we're unaware of just how much we know. This is the same for times table knowledge, number bonds, items of grammar, European capital cities, a basic chronology of British history, the ability to drive, or whatever else we might need to effortlessly recall.' Speaking fluent Mandarin would, colloquially, be called a skill. This example demonstrates that this skill is in fact the 'automatic and effortless' recall of a complex, embedded knowledge schema.

Expertise in any field relies upon schemas and procedural fluency. Leaders' expertise is no different. When we see a leader acting with skill, competence and deftness, what is invisible to us is the conceptual schema upon which they fluently draw (what Ackerman[7] refers to as the 'Dark Matter' of intelligence – more of this later). And this schema is a vast web of interconnected knowledge relevant to the context, scope and nature of the task at hand. As Joe Kirby puts it, 'The more knowledge you have, and the more automatically you can access it, the easier you find it to remember new knowledge, and the faster your skills develop.'[8]

A schema is a theoretical construct that there is evidence to support, but this model will no doubt develop as we understand more about brain architecture. The idea of *procedural fluency* is also useful to us. Together, these concepts help us stay grounded as to what leadership skill actually is, and to avoid getting carried away with notions of generic skills which are abstract from what we actually know: I term these 'hollow skills'.

Armed with these concepts, one can imagine the mental schema and procedural fluency of the leader building as they learn more, and practise more, the specific tasks they need to perform, in the specific contexts within which they operate. The skills they display are grown in the compost of knowledge. Since my repeated experience of making redundancies, my mental schema for managing this complex task has expanded and strengthened. Each experience has differed in its scale and scope, taken place at different times and within varied social and cultural contexts. The knowledge I need is far more likely, now, to be in my head than on a page. This makes the process more efficient, but it also makes for improved decision making as the necessary knowledge can be brought into working memory when it is needed, to help critically evaluate alternative options.

Further benefits will be gained in managing complex problems through the development and use of heuristics: mental shortcuts which can be employed to help make decisions quickly.[9] Heuristics are believed to be context-specific, but in new situations, an individual may compare the present dilemma to a mental model built up through similar experiences in the past and draw on this knowledge to help make a decision as to how to proceed (known as the representative heuristic). Heuristics may offer a way of transferring learning from one situation to another, therefore may contribute to the illusion of generic skills. However, heuristics introduce biases into our thinking and, like any abstract model, will only be useful to the extent that situations are similar in nature. Heuristics will be considered further in Section 2 when we will look at the possibility of transference of skills between contexts.

Skills with substance

The definition of leadership skills as 'procedural fluency', made possible by the repeated practice of applying a relevant, sophisticated mental schema to real-world scenarios, points us clearly towards how we could become a better leader. Firstly, we need to know more useful things. Secondly, we need to put what we know into practice. We must come to rely not on our toolkit of skills, but on our schema of knowledge. As Mary Myatt puts it, 'When we take short-cuts with knowledge in order to move on to acquisition of skills, it is like expecting a cook to make a meal with only one ingredient. It takes a range of materials or ingredients to produce something worthwhile'.[10]

The death of hollow leadership skills

Belief in generic leadership skills will not die easily. The concept is appealing and there are vested interests. How comforting it is to claim superior strategic planning skills, excellence in people management or the ability to influence others. Where would the leader's CV be without such a list of claims?

But we must kill off the notion that leadership skills exist independently of the specific context within which we operate and the domain of knowledge upon which we base our expertise. I believe that this idea has contributed to a range of problems, including:

- Complacency (dare I say arrogance) by those who come to believe that they have 'mastered' leadership competencies.
- The fallacy of 'smooth transfer' – belief that a generic skills toolkit is possessed by the leader, who can draw on competence gained in one context with ease to solve problems in another.
- The rise of 'abstraction' in school leadership, by which I mean the tendency to base school management and improvement on abstract models and processes rather than basing decisions on a deep knowledge of the leadership domain (see Chapter 6).
- Effort spent honing generic leadership skills rather than gaining knowledge relevant to the leadership role being performed.
- The rise of the 'super head' (an example of 'hero leader' romanticism discussed in Chapter 5)
- Misdirection in school improvement efforts, including ineffective leadership development programmes.

Go back ten spaces

A dispiriting aspect of the concept of domain-specific skills is the fear that you may have to start again in developing expertise as you move between problems and contexts. If the skills you have worked on and honed are relevant only to the specific leadership task you were working on at the time, then the expertise you have developed in one context will not benefit you in another, where you may find yourself to be a relative novice.

To overcome this problem, or at least to lessen its effect, we would need to know that skills are transferable in some way from one context to the next. The concept of generic skills assumes 100% transfer, and we have good reason to question this assumption. However, if we could even achieve 20 or 30% transfer of our skills from one context to the next, it would feel more like going back ten spaces in the game than being sent back to Start. The question of transfer will be considered in Chapter 9.

Summary of chapter substance

■■■■■■■ **Substance (stuff)** What do we need to know?	Leadership skills do not exist separately from the specific domain-knowledge within which they were acquired. Skills are built on a mental schema and are, as a result, domain-specific. Thinking of skills as 'procedural fluency' means the development of leadership skills will arise from knowing more and practising applying this knowledge until it becomes automatic and effortless.
■■■■■■■ **Substance (significance)** Why is this important?	A belief in generic (hollow) leadership skills gives us a false sense of expertise and diverts attention from activities which will secure effective leadership actions.
■■■■■■■ **Substance (validity)** How do we know it to be true?	The field of cognitive science has raised significant doubts about the dominance of generic skills. Our understanding of memory and learning increasingly points towards the importance of a mental schema upon which practitioners draw, and of deliberate practice as the mechanism for developing procedural fluency.

Further reading

This chapter draws heavily on the field of cognitive science. I would recommend two books in particular as an introduction for readers unfamiliar with this field:

Willingham, D. T. (2009) *Why Don't Students Like School* (first edition). San Francisco, CA: Jossey-Bass.

Didau, D. (2019) *Making Kids Cleverer: A manifesto for closing the advantage gap.* Carmarthen, Wales: Crown House Publishing.

References

1. Tricot, A. and Sweller, J. (2014) 'Domain-Specific Knowledge and Why Teaching Generic Skills Does Not Work', *Educational Psychology Review* 26 (2) pp. 265-283.

2. Geary, D. C. (2008) 'An Evolutionary Informed Education Science', *Educational Psychologist* 43 (4) pp. 179-195.

3. Newell, A. and Simon, H. A. (1972) *Human Problem Solving.* Englewood Cliffs, New Jersey: Prentice Hall.

4. Youssef, A., Ayres, P. and Sweller, J. (2012) 'Using General Problem-Solving Strategies to generate Ideas in Order to Solve Geography Problems', *Applied Cognitive Psychology* 26 (6) pp. 872-877.

5. Simon, D. P. and Gilmartin, K. (1973) 'Simulation of Memory for Chess Positions', *Cognitive Psychology* 5 (1) pp. 29-46.

6. Didau, D. (2018) 'How to explain... Schema', *The Learning Spy* [Online], 31 October. Retrieved from: www.bit.ly/2pKyWLE

7. Ackerman, P. L. (2000) 'Domain-Specific Knowledge as the "Dark Matter" of Adult Intelligence: Gf/Gc, Personality and Interest Correlates', *Journal of Gerontology* 55B (2) pp. 69-84.

8. Kirby, J. (2013) 'What can science tell us about how pupils learn best?'. *Pragmatic Reform* [Online], 23 March. Retrieved from: www.bit.ly/2pS9STa

9. Tversky, A. and Kahneman, D. (1974) 'Judgement Under Uncertainty: Heuristics and Biases', *Science* 185 (4157) pp. 1124-1131.

10. Myatt, M. (2018) *The Curriculum: Gallimaufry to Coherence.* Woodbridge: John Catt Educational.

Chapter 3
Do we need clever leaders?

'Who is the more foolish: the fool,
or the fool who follows him?'
– Obi-Wan Kenobi, *Star Wars: A New Hope* (1977)

We like our leaders to be smart. After all, we are (actually or metaphorically) following them into battle. We need to be confident that they have thought this through; that they are one step ahead of us, and of the other army's commander. As Obi-Wan implies, only the foolish follow a fool.

When we are asked to consider the traits a leader must possess, intelligence repeatedly comes out on top. In a study by Lord, Foti and De Vader,[1] subjects were asked which of a list of 59 characteristics (such as honesty, charisma and kindness) should be possessed by leaders. Intelligence not only emerged as the most defining characteristic of a leader, but the only attribute that must be possessed by all leaders. Reviews of the literature in the field also support this finding: intelligence is inextricably linked, in our minds, with strong leadership. A meta-analysis carried out by Lord, De Vader and Alliger[2] found intelligence to be correlated more strongly with leadership than five other key traits: masculinity-femininity, adjustment, dominance, extroversion-introversion and conservatism (a correlation of 0.50, for those who like numbers).

Reading through the research on people's perceptions of leaders, I am particularly struck by two things. Firstly, the fact that two researchers called Lord and De Vader worked together in the year that *Return of the Jedi* was released! Secondly, and probably more pertinent to the topic of this chapter, an interesting Gallup Poll from the 2000 presidential election saw 90% of Americans agree that 'understanding complex issues' was extremely or very important in determining which candidate they would vote for.[3] Now, in the light of recent events in American politics, either views about the importance of presidents being intelligent have changed, or US voters have a different view of Trump's IQ than I do. It turns out that both are true. In a 2018 Gallup Poll, 58% of Americans characterised President Trump as intelligent.[4] There are limited historic comparisons for this data, but Gallup did ask a similar question in the 1990s concerning President Clinton and H. W. Bush, who both scored higher. So, although Trump's IQ is not rated as highly as some other past presidents, a majority of the American public believe he's a clever guy.

Do intelligent presidents make the best presidents? In 2006, psychologist Dean Keith Simonton tried to answer this question by estimating the IQ of the first 42 U.S. presidents using data which is known to correlate, such as college entrance scores, level of education and occupation.[5] He then compared these estimates to a measure of 'presidential greatness' based on multiple ratings of leadership ability and found that the smarter the president, the better their ranking as a leader.* It would appear, then, that the cleverest presidents are also considered to be the best presidents. However, this research is retrospective; what we do not know is whether intelligence played a part in the election of these presidents in the first place. Given that the estimates of IQ in the study ranged from 118 (around the average for a college graduate) to 165 (well beyond genius), we can surmise that above-average intelligence either helped them get elected, was valued by the electorate, or both.

Smart, but not too smart

Think about your boss. And the boss above them. How intelligent are they?

---

* To save you looking it up, the three smartest presidents were found to be John Quincy Adams, Thomas Jefferson and John F. Kennedy.

We've established that we like our leaders to be clever, but how clever? The answer may be 'just a bit cleverer than us'. If we perceive ourselves to be more intelligent than those in charge, we might find ourselves questioning their decisions and wondering if we might actually do a better job. Once we question a leader's credibility, we are less likely to be influenced by them, and might even openly question their decisions. However, if our boss is operating at an intellectual level way above our heads, other problems may occur. We might feel intimidated by them, fail to make a social connection or simply not understand anything they are saying. The stereotype of the cold, isolated genius has some basis in truth; we probably all know someone we class as super-intelligent but who appears to be on another planet. There appears to be a 'Goldilocks zone' for intelligence, with our superiors being not too smart, but smart enough.

In a paper titled 'Can super smart leaders suffer from too much of a good thing?', John Antonakis, Robert J. House and Dean Keith Simonton set out to test four factors, which affect how intelligent we might want our leaders to be:[6]

1. **Diminishing returns on intelligence:** The smarter a leader is, 'the more this individual will be perceived as an optimal problem solver by others'. However, this advantage lessens as intelligence increases beyond a certain point.

2. **Comprehension factor:** 'Too large a gap between the intellectual inferiors and the leader reduces the leader's ability to influence because intellectual inferiors may not comprehend the message or the solutions proposed by the leader'.

3. **Criticism factor:** 'A leader of a group must have a sufficient level of intelligence so as not to be challenged by others who could appear to be more competent'. There is a trade-off between this and the previous factor: the leader needs to be sufficiently intelligent to avoid challenge, but not so intelligent that they leave others confused.

4. **Intellectual stratification:** The optimal level of intelligence will be related to 'the average intelligence of the group being led'.

Antonakis et al (2017) conclude (at the risk of over-simplifying) that leaders should have above average intelligence and an IQ of around 18 points above the mean of the group being led. They also assert that if the group's emphasis is more on social-emotional goals, then the IQ gap should be smaller, as it is more important that the leader is accepted as 'one of the team'. However, if the group's emphasis is more task-oriented, the IQ gap should be larger, as this will mean greater confidence in the leader to solve complex problems.

Evidence appears to support anecdote when it comes to how intelligent we want our leaders to be; smart, but not too smart. To return to our presidential example, while the retrospective view confirms that the more intelligent the president, the more successful we deem they are, when it comes to electing presidents, the American public don't usually go for the smartest.[7] If we were cynical, we might suggest that we prefer leaders with whom we can relate, over those who might be the most effective at doing the job. Gibb (1969) puts this sentiment well when he says, 'The evidence suggests that every increment of intelligence means wiser government, but that the crowd prefers to be ill-governed by people it can understand.'[8]

Never mind what we want; what do we need?

When I find myself in the position of looking to appoint a leader within my school, I am likely to pay some regard to how intelligent the candidates appear to be. I will have my own views on the importance of intelligence in leadership and the evidence above would suggest that I need to pay regard to the perceptions of those who will be led by the individual. However, short of giving applicants an IQ test (possible, but not often used in schools), how do I tell if individuals are clever enough to lead? Furthermore, can I be sure that an intelligent leader will actually deliver the goods?

The problem with many of the studies in this field, including all those cited above, is that they look at the *perceptions* of whether intelligence is important in leadership, not the reality. Determining whether intelligent leaders *are* more effective leaders is much more difficult, not least because leadership has no agreed definition, as discussed in Chapter 1. For this reason, the studies, which are often cited to support the view that intelligence is an important trait for leadership effectiveness, are often in the field of occupational performance. For example, a review of research by Schmidt and Hunter (1998)[7] found a strong correlation (0.51) between intelligence and general job-performance, which is stronger still for complex tasks. Others have made the theoretical case that the tasks that leaders do are intellectual functions, many of which are 'similar or identical to those we find on typical intelligence tests' (Fiedler and Garcia, 1987).[9] This all feels very unsatisfactory as an evidence base, appearing to say no more than 'leaders do difficult jobs; you need to be intelligent to do difficult things, therefore leaders must be intelligent'.

There is not yet enough research into the link between intelligence and leadership effectiveness to draw any firm conclusions, but a meta-analysis published in 2004 found a relatively weak correlation (0.21), suggesting that 'the relationship between intelligence and leadership is considerably lower than previously thought'.[10] Interestingly, the link between personality and leadership was found to be much stronger (with a correlation of 0.48), leading the authors to suggest that 'selecting leaders on the basis of personality appears to be relatively more important' (than intelligence). However, despite the modest influence of intelligence on leadership effectiveness, an effect does appear to exist and should not be dismissed. Judge et al make this important point:

> One possible explanation for the relatively modest relationship is that traits combine multiplicatively in their effects on leadership. It is possible that leaders must possess the intelligence to make effective decisions, the dominance to convince others, the achievement motivation to persist and multiple other traits if they are to emerge as a leader or be seen as an effective leader. If this is the case, then the relationship of any one trait with leadership is likely to be low. For example, it may be that high levels of intelligence will lead to high levels of leadership only if the individual also possesses the other traits necessary for leadership.

As suggested previously, leadership is a loose theoretical construct and cannot be defined simply (if at all); it is therefore unlikely to be correlated with one (or even a small number) of human traits or characteristics. Even if it were, it would be hard to establish the relationship between cause and effect.

It should also be remembered that this effect is an average, and that intelligence will be more important for some leaders than others. We have already noted that intelligence is more strongly correlated with complex tasks in the workplace, and it seems likely that leaders who undertake such tasks (such as constructing a timetable) will need a higher level of intelligence. It has also been suggested that higher levels of intelligence will have a greater impact on organisational effectiveness when the leader is directive, rather than participative, as their intelligence will more directly affect task performance.[11] Our experience as leaders might confirm this, as we may feel that our impact is limited by the effectiveness of those we lead; particularly in the context of schools, where leadership styles are more likely to be consultative, democratic or *laissez-faire*.

A last mitigating factor worth mentioning, as it is one that is particularly pertinent for schools, is the effect that workplace stress has on limiting the leader's ability to use their intelligence to achieve organisational goals.[12] Stress diverts a leader's 'attentional resources' away from tasks like planning and problem solving, and towards avoidance of failure, anxiety and self-doubt. If we wish to cultivate strong leadership in schools, we should be mindful of whether leaders' jobs are achievable.

What are the practical implications for schools?

What have we learnt about leadership that may help us as school leaders? The answer is not very much *of substance*. We may summarise the relevant findings from the research on the subject of intelligence and leadership as follows:

- We like our leaders to be intelligent, but not a lot more intelligent than us.
- Leaders of above average intelligence will do a marginally better job, on average, but this is not the most important characteristic for effective leaders.
- Intelligence is probably more important when the job involves highly complex tasks, or the leader is required to be decisive and directive.
- We can make intelligence work better for us if we do not put leaders under excessive stress.

- Leaders might be most effective when they combine intelligence with a range of other aptitudes.

This '*intelligence +*' view of leadership, whereby we want our leaders to be intelligent but to possess this quality alongside many others, in particular certain personality traits, is not all that surprising when we consider what intelligence is. Many have tried to define the concept of general intelligence, but an interesting definition in relation to this discussion is that 'intelligence measures an agent's ability to achieve goals in a wide range of environments'.[13] Or, as the journalist David Adam puts it, 'using what you've got to get what you want' (cited in Didau, 2019). What strikes me about this catchy phrase is that it only takes the addition of three words for it to be a fairly good definition of leadership… 'using what you've got to *get others to* get what you want'. The difference between the two definitions sheds light on why intelligence and leadership only correlate to an extent. The clever leader is only able to use their smarts to influence others. This insight corresponds to our understanding of the importance of personality in leadership and also to the apparently stronger link between intelligence and leadership when the leader is performing a complex task themselves (i.e. not through others) or is being directive (cutting out the problem of influencing others and making a path straight from the leader's intelligence to the desired outcome).

Beyond general intelligence

If, as I do, you remain dissatisfied with the usefulness of the research into intelligence as it pertains to leadership, perhaps it is because we have failed to move beyond a general view of intelligence. Might there be something of more substance if we dig a little deeper?

David Didau, in his 2019 book *Making Kids Cleverer*, deconstructs the concept of intelligence in an attempt to establish whether it is something we can actually improve.[14] He uses a definition of intelligence given by the researcher James Flynn, who breaks intelligence down into the following factors:[15]

- Mental acuity: the ability to come up with solutions to problems about which we have no prior knowledge.
- Speed of information processing: how quickly we assimilate new data.

- Habits of mind: the ways in which we are accustomed to using our minds.

- Attitudes: how the society in which we live tends to view and think about the world.

- Memory: our ability to retrieve information when it will be useful.

- Knowledge and information: the more you know, the more you can think about.

The first two (mental acuity and speed of information processing), Didau argues, are 'probably not amenable to being improved through social or educational intervention. That is to say, what you've got is all you'll ever have'. Social attitudes, on the other hand, may change but tend to do so slowly and this is not within the control of the individual. Habits of mind are cited as an aspect of intelligence that can be cultivated. The example given is the improvements in completing a cryptic crossword which will be gained by learning the patterns and hidden rules inherent in the task. However, it is the final two features of intelligence which Didau points to as the most important in making kids cleverer: the role of memory and the importance of expanding the quality and quantity of knowledge held in long-term memory. He puts it thus:

> The quantity and quality of what children know is, I believe, the most important individual difference between them. Those who know more are, on average, cleverer than those who know less. Although we might perceive some children to be more 'able' than others, this is unimportant because there's not really anything we can do about it. We can, however, do an awful lot about developing the quantity and quality of what children know.

Didau's claims are supported by the work of psychologist Richard Cattell[16] who, in the 1940s, proposed that intelligence should be separated into fluid and crystallised intelligence. Fluid intelligence is the reasoning power we use to solve problems which do not require prior knowledge (think of the sort of questions you would typically see on an IQ test: spatial awareness, logic) and is associated with concepts of working memory and task-focus. Crystallised intelligence is our ability to retrieve knowledge from long-term memory to inform our thinking, giving us something to think *about*. The significance of these concepts of intelligence is that fluid intelligence appears to be relatively fixed over time and resistant to change, whereas crystallised intelligence is eminently malleable. In short, if we want to become cleverer, our best bet is to improve the quantity and quality of what we know.

In terms of making kids (or anyone, we can presume) cleverer, Didau summarises his position thus:

1. Knowledge is what we think both with and about.

2. We cannot think with or about something we don't know.

3. The more we know about something, the more sophisticated our thinking.

If correct, we may conclude from Didau's analysis that the way to become cleverer is to know more. Didau's manifesto is to make kids generally cleverer by knowing generally more stuff (although he argues it needs to be the *right* stuff).

My concern, however, is not to breed generally cleverer leaders but to develop *specifically* clever leaders. In other words, leaders who can think in more sophisticated ways about the actual challenges they face. To consider how this should be achieved, we need to move from a notion of general intelligence (g) to one of domain-specific intelligence (ds).

The 'dark matter' of adult intelligence

It is a sad fact that our physical peak comes so early in life: around our mid-twenties. Health is wasted on the young. After that point, it is all downhill. The same can be said of intelligence; according to the data we have, at least. Repeated tests demonstrate that the middle-aged are, on average, less intelligent than young adults. Folk psychology appears to support these findings. We all know that our minds slow down, particularly in old age, and we start to forget what we came into a room for. We also hear of the great break-throughs made by scientists and mathematicians barely out of university. The young mind seems more agile and prone to take intuitive leaps.

But consider for a moment who you would rather have leading your school: someone in their 20s, or 50s? While we may value the energy, limited commitments and fierce ambition of the former, most of us would choose the wisdom and accumulated expertise of the latter. This is because we instinctively know that leading a large organisation is complex and requires a great deal of knowledge – and not the type you get from reading a book. We don't need a headteacher with general knowledge, either. We're not recruiting them to our pub quiz team. The knowledge we know our school leaders will need is occupationally specific: an understanding of pedagogy; safeguarding children; behaviour management; the examination system; employment law; children's mental health and so on. Are we to accept that older leaders are less intelligent but compensate for this with their accumulated knowledge? To many, this doesn't feel right. If a leader is making better decisions, navigating through challenging problems more successfully and judging situations with greater skill, should we not consider them to be smarter than the novice leader?

To reconcile the apparent contradiction between what IQ tests tell us about intelligence fading with age and what we observe in occupational settings as leaders get older and wiser, we might question whether the measures we are using fail to value the things that make us smarter as we move through adulthood: 'domains that are not assessed by traditional measures' (Ackerman, 2000).[17] Ackerman coins the term 'dark matter' to describe these so-far undiscovered domains, taking the term from the scientific hypothesis that a significant amount of the matter in the known universe is hidden to us, but has profound effects on the matter we can observe. He hypothesises that the nature of the 'dark matter' of intelligence is domain-specific knowledge (which he defines as including knowledge associated with occupations), which differs from the 'kinds of general cultural knowledge assessed in traditional one-to-one IQ tests'.

Ackerman proposes that 'if adults are given credit for what they know... it will be possible to better assess individual differences in intelligence from a real-world perspective (e.g. improving prediction of academic occupational success'. Like Didau after him, and Cattell before him, Ackerman calls for greater attention to be paid to the role of knowledge in conceptions of intelligence. In doing so, we may find that intelligence does not, in fact, deteriorate throughout adulthood but instead changes in its nature, becoming more about knowledge possessed than the capacity to manipulate knowledge, more specific than general, and with greater real-world rather than abstract application.

Intelligence with substance

If our traditional measures of general intelligence underestimate the role that domain-specific knowledge plays in adult intelligence, perhaps there is a greater correlation between intelligence and leadership than we have been able to establish thus far. A measure of domain-specific intelligence (*ds*), rather than general intelligence (*g*) measure, which favours the fluid aspects of intelligence, might indicate that intelligence plays a significant role in leadership and occupational success. Ackerman puts it well when he states:

> Many intellectually demanding tasks in the real world cannot be accomplished without a vast repertoire of declarative knowledge and procedural skills. The brightest (in terms of IQ) novice would not be expected to fare well when performing cardiovascular surgery in comparison to the middle-aged expert, just as the best entering college student cannot be expected to deliver a flawless doctoral thesis defence, in comparison to the same student after several years of academic study and empirical research experience. In this view, knowledge does not compensate for a declining adult intelligence; it *is* intelligence!

Further research is needed before we over-turn more than a century of tradition around intelligence testing, and it will be a long time before we can hope to know whether a model which values domain-specific intelligence correlates better with leadership effectiveness than the general intelligence model. My guess is that it would, but in the meantime, I see no harm in valuing domain-specific knowledge – the crystallised aspect of intelligence that we know to be malleable – over fluid intelligence, which is not.

While we might desire generally intelligent leaders in our schools, we certainly need knowledgeable ones. The substance of intelligence is what counts; the domain-specific knowledge which enables us to handle complexity. Not only is crystallised intelligence important, but it is the only aspect of intelligence which is responsive to our efforts to improve it.

We are not all born Einsteins, but we can become better leaders by developing the aspect of intelligence which is within our control. After all, those we lead don't want us to be geniuses; they just want us to know what we are talking about.

Summary of chapter substance

■■■■■■■ **Substance (stuff)** What do we need to know?	We like leaders to be a little more intelligent than us, but general intelligence only makes a marginal difference to leader effectiveness by itself. However, traditional notions of intelligence may underestimate the importance of domain-specific knowledge and, as this is the part of intelligence we know we can improve, developing this aspect of intelligence is an achievable and worthwhile goal.
■■■■■■■ **Substance (significance)** Why is this important?	Schools can be assured that they don't need to appoint highly intelligent or gifted people, just develop knowledgeable ones.
■■■■■■ **Substance (validity)** How do we know it to be true?	The research base around leadership and intelligence is not robust and questions remain about whether traditional measures of IQ are adequate in measuring real-world intelligence for adults. However, we can be confident in our assertion that domain-knowledge is important and malleable, and this provides something concrete for us to work on.

References

1. Lord, R. G., Foti, R. J. and De Vader, C. L. (1984) 'A Test of Leadership Categorization Theory: Internal Structure, Information Processing, and Leadership Perceptions', *Organizational Behavior & Human Performance* 34 (3) pp. 343-378.

2. Lord, R. G., De Vader, C. L. and Alliger, G. M. (1986) 'A Meta-analysis of the Relation Between Personality Traits and Leadership Perceptions: An Application of Validity Generalization Procedures', *Journal of Applied Psychology* 71 (3) pp. 402-410.3

3. Hambrick, D. Z. (2015) 'How Smart Should the President Be?', *Scientific American* [Online], 26 May. Retrieved from: www.bit.ly/2AR62f8

4. Manchester, J. (2018) '58 percent say Trump is intelligent in Gallup poll', *The Hill* [Online], 25 June. Retrieved from: www.bit.ly/337bCGo

5. Simonton, K. (2006) 'Presidential IQ, Openness, Intellectual Brilliance, and Leadership: Estimates and Correlations for 42 U.S. Chief Executives', *Political Psychology* 27 (4) pp. 511-526.

6. Antonakis, J., House, R. J. and Simonton, D. K. (2017) 'Can super smart leaders suffer from too much of a good thing? The curvilinear effect of intelligence on perceived leadership behaviour', *Journal of Applied Psychology* 102 (7) pp. 1003-1021.

7. Simonton, K. (1988) 'Presidential Style: Personality, biography, and performance', *Journal of Personality and Social Psychology* 55 (6) pp. 928-936.

8. Gibb, C. A. (1969) 'Leadership', in Lindzey, G. and Aronson, E. (eds) *Handbook of Social Psychology* (pp. 205-282). Reading, MA: Addison-Wesley.

9. Fiedler, F. E. and Garcia, J. E. (1987) *New Approaches to Effective Leadership: Cognitive Resources and Organizational Performance.* New York, NY: Wiley.

10. Judge, T. A., Colbert, A. E. and Ilies, R. (2004) 'Intelligence and Leadership: A Quantitative Review and Test of Theoretical Propositions', *Journal of Applied Psychology* 89 (3) pp. 542-552.

11. Fiedler, F. E. and House, R. J. (1994) 'Leadership Theory and Research: A Report of Progress', in Cooper, C. L. and Robertson, I. T. (eds) *Key Reviews in Managerial Psychology: Concepts and Research for Practice* (pp. 97-116). Chichester: Wiley.

12. Fiedler, F. E. (1986) 'The Contribution of Cognitive Resources and Leader Behaviour to Organizational Performance', *Journal of Applied Psychology* 16 (6) pp. 532-548.

13. Legg, S. and Hutter, M. (2007) 'Universal Intelligence: A Definition of Machine Intelligence', *Minds and Machines* 17 (4) pp. 391-444.

14. Didau, D. (2019) *Making Kids Cleverer: A Manifesto for Closing the Advantage Gap* (first edition). Carmarthen, Wales: Crown House Publishing.

15. Flyn, J. R. (2007) *What is Intelligence? Beyond the Flynn Effect.* Cambridge: Cambridge University Press, pp. 53-54.

16. Cattell, R. B. (1971) *Abilities: Their Structure, Growth, and Action.* Boston, MA: Houghton Mifflin.

17. Ackerman, P. L. (2000) 'Domain-Specific Knowledge as the "Dark Matter" of Adult Intelligence: Gf/Gc, Personality and Interest Correlates', *Journal of Gerontology* Vol. 55B (2) pp. 69-84.

Chapter 4
Model leadership

The elusive theory of everything

For many decades, physicists have been on a quest for the one grand theory that unites Einstein's gravitation and quantum physics. The belief which underlies this quest is that the same laws must apply across the universe (or universes), from the micro to the macro; one set of equations which explains it all. The favoured contender for this is known as string theory – a mathematical model of sub-atomic particles which has yet to be verified by experimental observations. But the problem is that string theory comes in five different versions, each with explanatory power, but only within specific situations. No one has been able to unify these so that they make sense as a whole: one magnificent theory of life, the universe and everything.

In *The Grand Design*, physicists Stephen Hawking and Leonard Mlodinow suggest that alternative string theory models may be the best we can hope to achieve in seeking a unifying theory of everything.[1] If, they argue, we consider the models we create to explain the universe as just that, models, and do not pretend that these models actually represent reality, we are freed from the quest to find one model that predicts everything. Instead, we can be satisfied that the various models we develop each correlate to particular aspects of our observations of the universe and, to that extent, they serve a purpose.

By separating theoretical models from actual existence, Hawking and Mlodinow remove the need to claim that a model represents reality; only whether it agrees with observations. Therefore, it is not a problem if two alternative models both agree with observations, as one cannot be said to be more real than the other. Whichever model serves the purpose of the person using it is the one that can be used.

This is physics at its most pragmatic!

The theory of *something*

The rejection of a theory of everything might provide us with a good analogy for how we view leadership models. The repeated efforts to form one grand theory of leadership have merely resulted in the equivalent of multiple string theories, each appearing to explain *something* about what we observe in organisations, but none robust enough to make sense of all known circumstances. Perhaps this is because, as suggested in Chapter 1, 'leadership' is merely a human construct which has no equivalent in reality?

What if there is, in fact, no theory of everything when it comes to leadership; no set of rules which explain what leadership is? And this is not because we are not up to the task of discovering this model, but because there is no such thing, in reality, to be modelled?

If we could just accept that our models of leadership are just models – theoretical constructs which help us understand some aspects of organisational behaviour – we could be released from the quest for the holy grail and turn our attention to the pragmatic task of working out what we can about organisations, using the tools we have at our disposal which prove reliable. Where these models correlate with what we see, then we use them judiciously to help explain, predict and inform. Where they do not, we discard them in favour of a model which serves our needs better.[2]

The advantage that some of our leadership theories have is that they do appear to correspond to observed reality. This makes them useful as explanatory and predictive tools. However, although they mirror reality, they remain as mere representations of it. To what extent can we reliably use these models to inform leaders in their everyday practice?

Mapping the leadership territory

'All the most exciting charts and maps have places on them that are marked with **unexplored***.'*

– *Swallows and Amazons* by Arthur Ransome[3]

When I'm not writing, running a school or driving my daughters to dance lessons, I climb as many mountains as possible. The joys of walking in the British mountains include discovering new territory, exploring the uplands and going off-path; even getting lost. While this pastime isn't without its risks, the venture is made eminently safer with the help of a map. I love maps. They not only have utility, but they are things of beauty. A well-drawn map is simple, elegant and possesses great clarity, such that the skilled navigator can establish exactly where they are and are going next. Maps connect us to the landscape and make wild places accessible to all those who possess the knowledge of how to read cartologically.

In his book, *Mountains of the Mind*, Robert MacFarlane describes a history of the development of maps.[4] He explains how, on early European maps, mountains were shown as molehills, or rocks, festooned with monsters and fantastical beasts. 'Where knowledge faded out, legend began', MacFarlane states. Over time, these mythical creatures disappeared from maps, replaced by representations of what could actually be found in the vicinity. Abstract depictions of geographical features did not begin to appear until the 16th century and, until then, had been represented figuratively, observed from ground level rather than looking down from above. During the Renaissance, cartographers developed some of the representative techniques we still use today, including contour lines denoting steepness: an abstract method which places marks on a map which represent not objects in the landscape but the lie of the land itself. Maps thereby moved into the third dimension, creating imagined undulations to the trained mind, which helped the reader picture themselves travelling through the terrain. Maps began to show not just what was there, but what it would feel like to *be* there.

The story of maps has many similarities to the evolution of leadership theory, both being abstract models of their respective terrains. The concept of leadership emerged from managerial and administrative theories,[5] useful for understanding the technical processes superiors would need to oversee production. The 'on the ground' reality of business functions was explored and researched to help establish greater efficiency, working practices and production design (by the likes of Taylor[6] and other 'scientific management' proponents). Much of the landscape of what we now think of as leadership remained uncharted. Human relations were considered a transactional affair: a fair day's work for a fair day's pay. Greater knowledge of psychology started to fill the gaps in mapped terrain, and directive management concepts began to be replaced by ethical considerations about human needs and democratic values. Leadership theories, as constructs in the field became known, moved from the concrete to the abstract. Rather than practical time-and-motion studies, the complexity of human interactions and motivations meant grander visions were needed in relation to the charisma and characteristics required to transform organisations. A codified language emerged (vision, strategy, culture, group dynamics) and multiple theories hypothesised in attempts to chart the territory from above, providing a consistent framework by which the leader could imagine themselves into the 'role' of leader... the hero explorer. In mapping the leadership territory, we have moved inextricably closer to charting every geographical feature and route through the landscape. Our representation of leadership is as close as we can get to recreating what it feels like to actually walking the terrain.

But I've walked in those mountains and I've studied the theory. There is so much missing from our attempts to map the terrain of leadership. MacFarlane captures this sentiment well when he says:[4]

> A map can never replicate the ground itself. Often our mapping sessions would induce us to bite off more than we can chew. At home we would plot a route over terrain that would, in reality, turn out to be sucking bog, or knee-high heather, or a wide boulder-field thick with snow. Sometimes a landscape would caution us of the limits of the map's power... Maps do not take account of time, only of space. They do not acknowledge how a landscape is constantly on the move – is constantly revisiting itself. Watercourses are always transporting earth and stone.

Gravity tugs rocks off hillsides and rolls them lower down...
These are the dimensions of a landscape which go unindicated
by a map.

How many times have we, as leaders, plotted a course that would turn out
to be a metaphorical sucking bog or knee-high heather?

The best model of a cat is a cat

The scientist Norbert Weiner is attributed to the quote: 'the best model
of a cat is another, or preferably the same, cat'. Weiner was pointing
out that however sophisticated our scientific models become, they will
never capture the complex reality of the subject itself. In his paper on
the subject, written with fellow scientist Arturo Rosenbleuth,[7] the role
of models in science is set out and critiqued. The simplification and
abstraction from reality provided by a model is its power, and models
are a necessity in enabling humans to test their hypotheses about how
the universe works. Models enable us to isolate the variables we are
interested in, to disregard the 'noise' and zero in on the aspects which
we believe to be the essence of the structure examined. Sometimes the
model reduces scale, either physical (like our maps) or time (reducing
earth's existence as if it all happened within a 24-hour period). Other
models disregard physical nature entirely and abstract to an intellectual
level, representing reality through formula or postulates.

Once we have our model we can ask questions of it. What if? Why? What
we learn to be true in our model is then suggested to be true in the system
it represents, *ceteris paribus* (all else being equal). We can test out the
reliability of our theoretical construct in explaining and predicting, and
it may prove an accurate model for the subject of our study, but it will
always be a model of some part of the whole. It will never be the cat itself.

Proceeding with caution

Theories of leadership abound. How should we think of them? Our
understanding of the limits of theoretical models should make us
cautious:

- We should beware of leadership models which claim to be the theory of everything. Specific theories which attempt to explain certain aspects of leadership and organisational behaviour are more likely to serve a useful purpose and to be supported by evidence.

- We should be more confident of theory where there is evidence from within our field of practice (school leadership), particularly from within our own context (e.g. special, comprehensive or single-sex schools). Better still, we should look for evidence of the application of leadership within our own school, remembering Dylan Wiliam's observation that 'everything works somewhere, but nothing works everywhere'.[8]

- We should be mindful that models are simplifications and abstractions. There may be evidence to support correlation (for example, between leader characteristics and measures of success in the organisation), or even causation (for example, between a leader's behaviour and the impact this has on others), but these will not hold in all circumstances and can only be taken as a 'rule of thumb'.

- We should remember that the best model of a cat is the cat itself. If we want to know what works, we need to look at our own school and the leadership which emerges. Leadership theories may point us towards where to look, or provide a handrail to follow, but they cannot replace a deep knowledge of the reality of daily life in the school in which we work.

Let us pick up some of these points in relation to the leadership models which appear to have most supporting evidence in school contexts.

Seven strong claims about successful school leadership*

The evidence to support the various leadership theories which have been proposed over the years is variable. However, in a much-cited NCSL publication (authored by Kenneth Leithwood, Christopher Day, Pam Simmons, Alma Harris and David Hopkins),[9] seven 'strong claims' about successful school leadership are made following an extensive literature review. These are:

1. School leadership is second only to classroom teaching as an influence on pupil learning.

2. Almost all successful leaders draw on the same repertoire of basic leadership practices.

3. The ways in which leaders apply these basic leadership practices – not the practices themselves – demonstrate responsiveness to, rather than dictation by, the contexts within which they work.

4. School leaders improve teaching and learning indirectly and most powerfully through their influence on staff motivation, commitment and working conditions.

5. School leadership has a greater influence on schools and students when it is widely distributed.

6. Some patterns of distribution are more effective than others.

7. A small handful of personal traits explains a high proportion of the variation in leadership effectiveness.

Claim 1 sets the tone for the arguments which follow by placing leadership at second place in its influence on pupil learning, behind classroom teaching. The authors point to a review of large-scale quantitative studies between 1980 and 1998 which concludes that the effects of school leadership, both direct and indirect combined, are small but educationally significant, accounting for between 5 and 7% of the difference in pupil learning and achievement across schools. Many of these differences are attributed to pupil intake and demographic factors, but of the variables within a school's control, leadership accounts for around a quarter of the effects against a third for classroom factors. Rather than leadership being the direct cause of improved outcomes, Leithwood et al describe it as the 'catalyst without which other good things are quite unlikely to happen': the baking soda that helps the cake rise.

The remaining claims set out the evidence for how leadership impacts to the extent described, although the strength of evidence diminishes with each claim. Claim 2 draws on a synthesis of evidence collected from school and non-school contexts to propose four sets of 'leadership qualities and practices', which help improve employee performance that, in turn, is suggested to be a function of the employees' beliefs, motivations, skills and knowledge and the conditions in which they work. The four sets of qualities and practices are:

- Building vision and setting direction
- Understanding and developing people
- Redesigning the organisation
- Managing the teaching and learning programme.

Leithwood et al address the generic nature of the aforementioned by acknowledging the importance of the contexts within which leaders work, rejecting an absolute position that leadership is entirely context-specific and instead claiming that leaders apply qualitatively similar practices across different organisations and types of organisation. They emphasise how different practices will come to the fore in different contexts; for example in school-turnaround scenarios where the direction will be set centrally, radical and urgent restructuring occurs and particular types of teaching approaches will be insisted upon by school leaders. While leaders may influence curriculum and pedagogy directly in such circumstances, school leaders more commonly influence indirectly through creating the conditions in which employees subscribe to the school's goals and are equipped and motivated to help achieve them.

Lastly, the authors address the question of who we consider the leaders in a school to be, and what traits they must possess. The popular, but not fully substantiated, call for distributed leadership is found to be 'quite compelling', with one study concluding that the effect of the 'total leadership' within schools accounted for 27% of student learning and achievement effects; two or three times higher than typically reported studies of individual headteacher effects.[10] However, extremely limited evidence currently exists as to what pattern of distributed leadership is most effective in schools. The evidence for which traits leaders must possess is also limited; at least in relation to schools. The authors cite evidence in relation to studies of low-performing schools, which suggest that the traits of open-mindedness, flexible thinking, persistence, resilience and optimism are paramount in such contexts as leaders face the extremely challenging task of achieving improvement in almost impossible circumstances.

What should we take from these claims?

The strongest of the 'strong claims' made in this paper do indeed meet the call to be substantiated by school-specific evidence. Leaders in successful schools would appear to adopt a similar set of practices, although the application of these is acknowledged to vary between contexts. There is a bias in studies towards leadership practices in struggling schools, which is understandable as this is where evidence of 'what works' is most needed and there is a government social-justice agenda supporting this effort. This evidence often supports the efficacy of what might be termed 'transformational leadership' approaches, due to the urgent need to act and make rapid improvement, and this bias should be recognised before applying such practices in other contexts. Least convincing is the claim that certain leadership traits might be identified as consistently held by the most effective school leaders.

As a leader, what can I learn from this synthesis of the literature on school leadership, and how should I apply this? I might take confidence from the conclusion that leadership plays an important role in catalysing school improvement – it appears that it is worth me turning up every day! I also know that I need a little humility, as without classroom teachers, my effect will be limited. My role is to create the conditions for them to be effective and to allow others to lead, also. But what of the 'qualities and practices' which it is suggested I should adopt? How should I set about these tasks? How should I apply them to the context in which I work?

The authors claim that the proposed core practices 'provide a powerful new source of guidance for practising leaders, as well as a framework for initial and continuing professional development'. Do they?

There appears to me to be some misdirection in such claims; some sleight of hand which distracts us from where our attention might better be focused. To understand why this might be, consider how such frameworks are arrived at. The research methods employed in such studies are often correlational, i.e. they look at successful schools and school leaders and identify the behaviours they have adopted. In these studies, we must not be tempted to confuse the fact of coincidence with causation: that one or more factors is the cause of the success. Where studies attempt to establish causation, the evidence may be testimony by the leaders themselves, or others in the organisation. Furthermore, even where research is randomised and controlled, isolating specific behaviours as causal factors is challenging, at best. The meta-study approach taken by the authors of this publication helps give us greater confidence that the identified behaviours play some role in school effectiveness, but cannot fully overcome the limitations of social studies.

However, even if we can establish the importance of said behaviours with some confidence, what then do we make of this information in a practical sense? The tendency is to suggest that leaders must adopt these behaviours or be trained to become expert in them. It is as if we are being told, 'Look! This is what successful leaders do. If you can do as they do, your school will be successful too'. But is that how these leaders became successful themselves? Was their aim to develop particular traits or adopt a list of practices? To claim that the core practices set out should 'provide a powerful new source of guidance for practising leaders' is to assert something that we cannot be sure of, which is that what we observe in successful leaders are also the things we should focus on developing in ourselves.

Models of leadership may well be explanatory, and they may predict the outcome of certain actions, traits or behaviours by leaders. However, when we move from describing to prescribing, from clarity to advocacy, we exceed the limits of what our model is for. The frameworks developed by researchers can become heuristics, which we are encouraged to follow.[11] As such fashionable theories take hold, they can become a self-reinforcing loop. Leaders incorporate these ideas into their schema and vocabulary and begin to attribute their success to the application of such heuristics and the possession of the qualities advocated.[12] We come to believe that our success is attributable to the characteristics we are told make us successful. Remember that a model of a cat is just a model of a cat – we cannot use it to assert what a cat should be or how it has come to be that way.

It seems unlikely that we will land upon a model of leadership that explains everything we observe. We should be satisfied with an ever-evolving range of theories which can be applied selectively and cautiously to help understand this phenomenon within organisations, never forgetting that if we want to know how to lead, we should examine ourselves and understand the context within which we operate. Theories provide a framework for understanding, but they are abstractions from reality and can never truly capture the complexity and nuances of the school leadership terrain. When theoretical models lead to evangelical advocacy for particular forms of leadership, we should reject these and stay grounded in the reality of our school context.

Summary of chapter substance

▄▄▄▄▄▄▄ **Substance (stuff)** What do we need to know?	There is not, and might never be, a single, unified model of school leadership. We should seek out theories for which there is strong evidence and apply these selectively and cautiously to understand the context within which we lead. Leadership is important in schools, but not the most or only factor in success. We must lead with humility and sensitivity, taking the time to walk the terrain of our schools rather than rely on abstract notions of what success looks like.
▄▄▄▄▄▄▄ **Substance (significance)** Why is this important?	What leaders do makes a difference. However, schools change over time and no two schools are the same. We will not find the answers we need in a textbook or grand theory, but we can draw on the evidence we have to inform our practice.
▄▄▄▄▄▄▄ **Substance (validity)** How do we know it to be true?	The body of research into school leadership is growing, but there is plenty of uncharted territory. Our knowledge remains tentative and it is healthy to remember this.

Further reading

Bush, T. and Glover, D. (2014) 'School Leadership Models: What Do We Know?', *School Leadership & Management* 34 (5) pp. 1-19.

* Please note that the Leithwood et al publication was updated in 2019, prior to when this chapter was written. I have referenced the original paper as it illustrates the points I am making best and is the more commonly cited version of the paper. The updated version addresses some of the criticisms made in this chapter and acknowledges the importance of domain-specific knowledge in leadership. In the opinion of the author, the revised publication presents a more robust set of claims about leadership than the original.

References

1. Hawking, S. and Mlodinow, L. (2010) *The Grand Design*. New York, NY: Bantam Books.

2. Lambert, L. (1995) 'New Directions in the Preparation of Educational Leaders', *Thrust for Educational Leadership* 24 (5) pp. 6-10.

3. Ransome, A. (1930) *Swallows and Amazons*. London: Penguin.

4. MacFarlane, R. (2003) *Mountains of the Mind: A History of a Fascination*. London: Granta Publications.

5. Gunter, H. (2004) 'Labels and Labelling in the Field of Educational Leadership', *Discourse – Studies in the Cultural Politics of Education* 25 (1) pp. 21-41.

6. Much has been written about Taylor and the field of scientific management. The original publication on this subject is: Taylor, F. W. (1911) *The Principles of Scientific Management*. New York, NY: HarperCollins.

7. Weiner, A. and Rosenbleuth, N. (1945) 'The Role of Models in Science', *Philosophy of Science* 12 (4) pp. 316-321.

8. Wiliam, D. (2016) *Leadership for Teacher Learning*. Florida: Learning Sciences International.

9. Leithwood, K., Day, C., Sammons, P., Harris, A. and Hopkins, D. (2006) *Seven strong claims about successful school leadership*. National College for School Leadership and Department for Education and Skills. London: The Stationery Office.

10. Mascall, B. and Leithwood, K. (2008) 'Collective Leadership Effects on Student Achievement', *Educational Administration Quarterly* 44 (4) pp. 529-561.

11. Gunter, H. (2013) 'Distributed Leadership: A Study in Knowledge Production', *Educational Management, Administration and Leadership* 41 (5) pp. 555-580.

12. Lumby, J. (2013) 'Distributed Leadership: The Uses and Abuses of Power', *Educational Management, Administration and Leadership* 41 (5) pp. 581-597.

Chapter 5

Transient turnarounds

One of the interesting features of schools is that they are in a constant state of transformation. A significant reason for this is the steady turnover of students. For example, in an 11-16 secondary school, approximately one-fifth of the students will leave each year and a new cohort will join. This continuous change means that the ethos of a school must constantly be renewed and reset. Over a five-year period, the entire student population will have changed. In many settings, the continuity of schooling can be maintained by the staff, who are likely to turnover at a lower rate. In the school in which I currently work, the staff turnover rate is relatively low (at 5-10% each year), and there are a number of staff who have worked at the school for ten or more years. This provides the benefit of continuity and stability. However, in some schools, the staff will turnover at a similar rate to the students, and the leadership challenge will be to reset expectations and culture each year with a cohort of new staff, as well as new students.

I recently spoke with a headteacher of a new secondary school whose second cohort of students had just arrived. He spoke of the privilege of starting a school with a cohort of Year 7 students and a small, committed group of staff who were able to work closely to create the desired culture. When the second cohort arrived, it was not difficult to assimilate these new students into the school. However, what proved challenging was the influx of new staff; almost doubling the numbers employed the year before. These new staff threatened to overwhelm the culture which had developed among the founding group and, rather than be inducted into the established ways of doing things, brought their own standards and expectations, to the disgruntlement of the original group of staff. Although the circumstances of a new school are unique, this example illustrates the challenges faced by school leaders when both the student and staff profile rapidly transforms.

The transience of the student population and the turnover rates of staff are often highest in 'troubled' schools. I use the term 'troubled' rather than the more commonly used 'failing' deliberately, because schools branded as failing are frequently those facing the most challenging circumstances and are often doing a remarkable job of educating students against all odds. Achieving school improvement is all the more difficult when the school struggles to maintain consistency of staffing, and securing permanency of standards requires constant heroic efforts by school leaders and the staff who stay the course. Unfortunately, an improvement in educational outcomes can prove transitory and schools can easily find standards declining to previous levels. Securing sustained school improvement, particularly for troubled schools, is an urgent and high priority for our educational system, but a goal which proves elusive.

Under new management

Improving the lowest performing schools has been a political goal for some time. However, in 2000, the then Labour government created a new vehicle for school improvement in the form of sponsored academies; a legal structure by which under-performing local authority schools could be converted to state-funded, independent schools through investment and stewardship of private individuals or companies. This change signalled a renewed enthusiasm, on behalf of government, to tackle social disadvantage through the provision of education.

Over the next two decades, the academy model was extended across the education system such that, by 2019, the majority of pupils attending state-funded schools in England were on roll in an academy school, either a stand-alone entity or, increasingly, as part of a multi-academy trust (MAT). The proliferation of MATs was central to the coalition government's 2010 announcement of a 'self-improving school-led system',[1] which effectively meant that troubled schools could be re-brokered into a new MAT if the required improvement was not rapid or significant enough. These changes brought about an 'under new management' approach to school improvement, with the rebranding of schools taking place in the same way as a pub might be given a facelift by a new proprietor.

It is not the intention of this book to provide a detailed critique of government policy, but the changes described above are pertinent to our consideration of school leadership as they have increased the pressure on troubled schools to show rapid improvement, lest they face a management restructuring and change of ownership. This has been a significant factor in the approach leaders have taken to school improvement and the increase in superficial and transient measures and methods of school turnaround efforts.

Stepping up to the challenge of turning around under-performing schools came the 'trouble-shooter' headteachers, epitomised by Michael Wilshaw, Principal of Mossbourne Academy and later Chief Inspector of Schools at Ofsted. Wilshaw's leadership style has been described as combining the role of 'business executive, saviour, pioneering cowboy and military commander'.[2] Charismatic heads were heralded by politicians as figureheads for the new school system, able to single-handedly turn around the fortunes of generations of young people. A fetish for heroic school leaders made the mere mortals (the majority of those in charge of schools) appear complacent and weak. Schools which were not showing rapid improvement in results through radical management-imposed policies were branded as 'coasting' or 'requiring improvement'.

Transforming schools

This period in the history of schooling in the UK coincided with 'transformational leadership' becoming the dominant theoretical construct. An idea originally conceived of in the 1970s, transformational leadership gained credibility as empirical research increasingly found evidence of positive effects in organisations,[3] across industries[4] and at a national level,[5] correlating with improved productivity,[6] profit,[7] customer satisfaction,[8] innovation,[9] job satisfaction[10] and staff retention.[11]

Transformational leadership has been criticised as an ambiguous concept,[12] but Bass[13] provides a useful framework for understanding transformational leadership as composing of four inter-connected components:

1. **Charisma:** the personal magnetism that attracts people to follow.

2. **Intellectual stimulation:** an ability to focus people's minds on problems and finding solutions.

3. **Individualised consideration:** the tendency to recognise the potential of the individual and help them achieve their potential.

4. **Inspirational leadership:** the ability to arouse followers' emotions.

Employing these four characteristics, transformational leaders lift followers above their narrow self-interests to become selfless and motivated in achieving radical change. This notion of leadership has promoted the idea of leaders presenting a compelling vision which followers are morally motivated to work towards, giving an organisation a shared sense of purpose and identity.[14]

Transformational leadership appears to fit well with the moral crusade of 'rescuing' failing schools and the vulnerable and disadvantaged pupils within them. Teachers, by the fact that they have chosen the profession, are already primed for selfless service towards a moral imperative, and those drawn to schools in disadvantaged areas possibly even more so. Given a charismatic leader they can believe in, and the opportunity to make a real difference to generations of young people, schools under such leadership appear set to attract and retain the highest calibre of professionals. The transformational leadership model seems ideal for a system that seeks to disrupt the status quo and rapidly raise educational outcomes.

Superficial transformation

On paper, it would appear that we have the perfect model for raising educational standards, particularly where there has been a history of under-performance and disadvantage: schools have been liberated from the bureaucracy of local authority control; heroic leaders appointed with a moral mission to turn around the school; additional resources directed to where the greatest challenges exist; pressure exerted to engender a sense of urgency. However, the calibration of this system was not quite right.

To understand where this model for system improvement may have gone wrong, we should consider the incentives and disincentives built into the model and their effect on leadership behaviour.

The first question a school improvement method must address is what does improvement look like, and how will we know when it has been achieved? We have a ready-made measure for this purpose in the form of school league tables. Of course we know that examination results are not the only, or even a particularly reliable, indicator of educational quality, but they stand as the best proxy we have for school standards. Examination results are the visible indicator of the quality of education a student has received over the past 11 years of formal education. A genuinely improved educational experience would see exam results increase due to the raised quality of every stage of schooling, from Reception to Year 11. The exam results would be the indicator of this success, not the object.

However, with the pressure to rapidly improve troubled schools, leaders naturally set about finding quick, high impact ways to increase results. There is a strong moral case for doing so: we cannot wait 11 years and condemn numerous cohorts of students before we achieve improved outcomes. The moral duty for school leaders in such circumstances is to balance the immediate, short-term problem of helping students achieve better results now with the longer-term objective of alleviating the need for short-term fixes in the future. The problem for school leaders has been that the incentives are heavily weighted towards prioritising short-term fixes as rapidly improved exam results are met with heroic status, plaudits and improved finances as the school attracts higher numbers of students. To compound this problem, the sanctions for failing to show rapid improvement, including suffering the indignity of a takeover and the headteacher probably losing their job, are severe.

It is no wonder that, in the face of such pressures, schools turned to any and every method possible to increase exam results. Intensive one-to-one interventions became the norm in many schools, and teachers were increasingly 'asked' to provide extra classes after school and during the school holidays. Significant additional funding provided through the pupil premium initiative incentivised resource-intensive strategies, ensuring there was no excuse for schools not to throw everything at achieving better grades. The proliferation of qualification types during this period (which we shall discuss further in Chapter 11) enabled schools to shop around for the easiest path for students to achieve the required grades. The result was an apparent rapid transformation in some schools, which fed the rhetoric of heroic leadership even further. Schools in less difficult circumstances found their positions in league tables begin to fall if they too were not employing the 'raising achievement' strategies, and many began to mimic the 'good practice' publicised through Ofsted reports and the media (see the next chapter for an analysis of this process). In this way, examination success became a goal in itself, regardless of the means by which improvement was achieved.

It became increasingly difficult for leaders to maintain integrity during this period. The idealised model of the transformative leader in some cases gave way to the unethical alter-ego, labelled by Bass as 'pseudo-transformational'; a claimed moral purpose hiding a wilful disregard for moral means. The effects of this failed model of educational improvement are still being felt in the form of excessive workload, low morale, teacher shortages, high exclusion rates and 'off-rolling' of pupils who will bring down the school's results. Ironically, rather than helping to overcome the difficulties caused by transience in staffing, many struggling schools have become reliant on a constant churn of staff who burn brightly, but burn out quickly, driven away not by the challenges presented by the school's context but by the demands placed on them by school leaders.

New vocabulary provides an indicator of cultural change, and the term 'toxic schools' entered the lexicon of those in the profession. Who would have imagined that schools could become so poisonous to those committing themselves to such a noble vocation as teaching?

Detoxifying our schools

It is easy to lay the blame for the recent failures of the school system at the door of government and Ofsted. However, apportioning blame will not solve the problem, and school leaders must accept their share of both the responsibility for the current situation and finding solutions.

The starting point is to question some of the conventional wisdom which has grown up around school improvement efforts and to ensure that integrity is at the heart of school leadership. Here are some questions leaders should be asking themselves right now:

- Do we view examination results as one, flawed proxy for a good education or as an end in themselves?
- Aside from exam certificates, what are students at my school walking away with?
- Are resources equally employed across each year group?
- Is my school a place where people want to stay and develop their careers?
- Would I want to work in a non-leadership position in my school?
- Do our school improvement efforts rely on unreasonable levels of work for staff?
- Has the improvement in my school become unhealthily reliant on my personal effort, charisma and resilience?
- Am I a model of humility and fallibility for those around me?
- To what extent are my decisions as a leader driven by external incentives and threats, rather than by the needs of the community I serve?
- Do school improvement strategies rely on doing more things, rather than doing fewer things, better?
- How do we ensure permanent, rather than transient, change in our school?

The national framework for school improvement is just one factor that has led school leaders to prioritise superficial notions of quality over strategies that might actually improve educational standards. In the next chapter, we will consider the role Ofsted have played in spreading genericism in schools, and the managerialist response of school leaders, which has undermined the role of professional expertise within our school system.

Summary of chapter substance

■■■■■■■ **Substance (stuff)** What do we need to know?	Improving schools takes time, and although there is an urgency to secure a better education for the children receiving their education now, this should not lead to prioritising superficial success over meaningful and lasting improvement. As school leaders, we play an important role in facilitating change, but we should not surrender our integrity or portray ourselves as something we are not.
■■■■■■■ **Substance (significance)** Why is this important?	Setting a false expectation for what schools can achieve within a reasonable timescale does no favours for pupils, staff or school leaders. Permanent change is best achieved by ensuring worthwhile endeavours and sustainable efforts.
■■■■■■ **Substance (validity)** How do we know it to be true?	Toxic school cultures, staff shortages and high workloads are the result of a failed model for improving educational standards over the last two decades. There is a growing consensus that our system needs fewer heroes and more sustainable approaches to improving the quality of education.

References

1. University of College London (2018) 'Chaotic' Government Reforms are Failing to Tackle Education Inequality', *Institute of Education* [Online]. Retrieved from: www.bit.ly/2ALc6Gb

2. Kulz, C. (2015) 'Heroic Heads, Mobility Mythologies and the Power of Ambiguity', *British Journal of Sociology of Education* 38 (2) pp. 85-104.

3. Nemanich, L. A. and Keller, R. T. (2007) 'Transformational Leadership in an Acquisition: A Field Study of Employees', *Leadership Quarterly* 18 (1) pp. 49-68.

4. Garcia-Morales, V. J., Jimenez-Barrionuevo, M. M. and Gutierrez-Gutierrez, L. (2012) 'Transformational Leadership Influence on Organizational Performance through Organizational Learning and Innovation', *Journal of Business Research* 65 (7) pp. 1040-1050.

5. Howell, J. M. and Avolio, B. J. (1993) 'Transformational Leadership, Transactional Leadership, Locus of Control, and Support for Innovation: Key Predictors of Consolidated-Business-Unit Performance', *Journal of Applied Psychology* 78 (6) pp. 891-902.

6. Ibid.

7. Hofman, D. A. and Jones, L. M. (2005) 'Leadership, Collective Personality, and Performance', *Journal of Applied Psychology* 90 (3) pp. 509-522.

8. Liao, H. and Chuang, A. (2007) 'Transforming Service Employees and Climate: A Multilevel, Multisource Examination of Transformational Leadership in Building Long-Term Service Relationships', *Journal of Applied Psychology* 92 (4) pp. 1006-1019.

9. Garcia-Morales, V. J., Jimenez-Barrionuevo, M. M. and Gutierrez-Gutierrez, L., (2012) 'Transformational Leadership Influence on Organizational Performance through Organizational Learning and Innovation', *Journal of Business Research*, 65 (7) pp. 1040-1050.

10. Braun, S., Peus, C., Weisweiler, S. and Frey, D. (2013) 'Transformational Leadership, Job Satisfaction, and Team Performance: A Multilevel Mediation Model of Trust', *Leadership Quarterly* 24 (1) pp. 270-283.

11. Tse, H. H. M., Huang, X. and Lam, W. (2013) 'Why Does Transformational Leadership Matter for Employee Turnover? A Multi-foci Social Exchange Perspective', *Leadership Quarterly* 24 (5) pp. 763-776.

12. Lee, M. (2014) 'Transformational Leadership: Is It Time For A Recall?', *International Journal of Management and Applied Research* 1 (1) pp. 17-29.

13. Bass, B. M. and Riggio, R. E. (2006) *Transformational Leadership*. London: Routledge.

14. Burns, J. M. (1978) *Leadership*. New York, NY: Harper and Row.

Chapter 6
Abstraction and distraction

'Mind-forg'd manacles'
- *London* by William Blake

When I became a headteacher in 2013, my boss at the time gave me a book called *Brave Heads: How to Lead a School Without Selling Your Soul*.[1] The message of the book was not to give in to the pressures placed on you to chase exam results but instead stick to what you believed to be right: values over performance measures.

I didn't need much encouragement, to be honest. I was born with a natural tendency to be contrary (note that my blog is called *TheEduContrarian*). When asked to do something, my instinct is to do the opposite. Therefore, I set out to run a school in the way I believed a school should be run and not in the way others expected me to.

In 2013, there were many (in my opinion) dubious practices going on in our schools. Triple-impact marking was all the rage; teachers would be regularly observed and their lessons graded, data collection took place up to six times a year and Easter revision courses for GCSE students were on the increase. I felt uneasy with all of these practices and questioned whether I wanted the school I ran to be part of the orthodoxy of the time. I had tentatively started acquainting myself with research in education through the gateway drug of John Hattie's *Visible Learning.*[2] Twitter, which I had been using as a teaching tool for my A Level economics students, connected me to a community of teachers and leaders, many of whom were even more contrary than I. David Didau asked, what if everything I knew about teaching was wrong?[3] I set about finding out.

In the years that followed, I took away many of the things I felt were just getting in teachers' way. I wanted the school in which I was headteacher to be one in which I would be happy to work in any other position, and a school I would be pleased for my own children to attend. I've always wanted to do a great job and be trusted to get on with it; the starting point for me is assuming that others feel the same. People need support, but they don't need to be micro-managed. As for the students, well, nobody wants their children taught by tired and miserable teachers. By and large, this formula worked and the school improved in so many ways. Staff sickness levels fell, morale improved, results increased and more parents started sending their children to the school.

Then, in 2017, Ofsted downgraded the school from 'good' to 'requires improvement'. They acknowledged that the school had made significant improvements, results had risen, we had closed the attainment gaps for disadvantaged children, leadership was strong, there were high standards of behaviour and pastoral care was good. They commented that the parent survey was one of the best they had seen in any school for years. However, they'd seen a few dodgy lessons and weren't happy that the pupils' books 'showed enough progress'. We hadn't been able to provide the data they wanted to see ('something like a flight-path', one inspector requested). We hadn't been able to provide the evidence to 'prove' that what they had observed was not typical. We were shocked and devastated: staff, governors, pupils and parents alike. What they described in the report felt nothing like the school we knew.

Salvaging something from the wreckage

At exactly the same time as we were being interrogated by inspectors, Professor Rebecca Allen was delivering a lecture,[4] the transcript of which I read in the days after our Ofsted inspection. What she said resonated with me at the time in a way that little has done, before or since. Struggling to face the staff meeting with something encouraging to say, I shared the essence of this lecture to help explain what had just happened and how we should respond.

In her lecture, Rebecca Allen described what she termed the 'audit culture' which has developed in England's schools which, over time, has 'displaced the culture of trust and of teaching as a private endeavour'. To understand how this culture has emerged, Allen draws on the work of two sociologists, Paul DiMaggio and Walter Powell,[5] who developed a framework for describing how apparently independent organisations all come to resemble each other; a process they call institutional isomorphism.

The framework includes three 'forces' which, when applied to the English education system, work like this:

1. **Coercive isomorphism**

   This is where the threat of inspection and scrutiny forces schools to fall in line with a particular model of what effective schools look like. Allen cites an example of a school which had not been inspected since 2008, and yet many of the school's policies emphasise how the school would look to 'a visitor'. She argues that an important factor in this behaviour was the change from long to short inspections by Ofsted in 2005. Allen states that 'once this happened, it became impossible to do little more than use the inspection to check the headteacher had sufficient written evidence to support their own self-evaluation form. For headteachers who needed to prove that they knew their school's strengths and weaknesses, this resulted in a cascade of school policies to mirror what the senior leadership team estimated Ofsted would be looking for.'

2. **Mimetic isomorphism**

   To manage the risk of inspection, schools look to each other to mimic the practices of good and outstanding schools. Where this results in the sharing of good practices this is helpful, but DiMaggio and Powell contend that it often causes the spread of ineffective practice where it is difficult to prove the efficacy of these ideas. Allen points out that mimicking the behaviour of the majority of schools is safer, as 'if the herd makes the wrong decision about which way to run, it is still safer to be nestled in the middle of the herd.'

3. Normative isomorphism

Our professional identity as teachers and leaders defines what we do, and this identity is heavily influenced by the prevailing norms in the education system as to what good teachers/leaders/schools do. We all know that teachers work long hours, take home piles of books to mark, differentiate work for children, 'control' bad behaviour and do anything they can to make a child's life better. Equally, we know that school leaders enforce standards, hold teachers to account, monitor the quality of lessons, scrutinise exercise books, raise results and maximise the school's chance of a good inspection outcome. These are the 'mind forg'd manacles' to which Blake refers, quoted at the start of this chapter.

What resonated with me about Allen's application of DiMaggio and Powell's work is that it described everything I had set out not to do in my school. My aim was to *'be* good' rather than *'look* good'. To do this, I would make our school *different* to many others I had seen, not the same. There was much to admire about what was happening in other schools, but I felt it as important to learn from others' mistakes as much as their successes. Lastly, I rejected the expectations of the education system about what a good school should be. Success, in my mind, is about standing out from the crowd, not fitting in. Was I a 'Brave Head' or a dangerous renegade? I felt hoisted by my beliefs; punished for my unorthodoxy.

Rebecca Allen's words made me question whether I belonged to a different era of leaders:

Now let us turn to the normative forces that define what it means to be a school leader today. Today's headteachers have often cut their managerial teeth in a period in which good leaders are those who regularly collect evidence that standards are being met in each of their classrooms week-in, week-out. Governors, parents, trades unions, professional development organisations and local authority networks all serve to reinforce these normative views of what constitutes high professional standards in leadership. By contrast, many – though not all – of the headteachers who upheld very different conceptions of what it means to be a teaching leader have long since chosen to leave the profession. And the teachers who don't want to subscribe to the audit culture find they cannot be promoted to leadership positions.

The prevailing norms of school leadership seem to me to be distracting leaders (and therefore teachers) from doing the things which will actually make a difference to children's education. Worse still, in some schools and trusts, it has become almost intolerable for teachers and leaders with integrity (and a life outside of school) to carry on. But it isn't only Ofsted that distracts us from meaningful endeavour.

Managerialism

The practices in today's schools which I instinctively dislike seem to be symptomatic of an approach to leadership known as managerialism, which may be described as follows:

> Managerial leadership assumes that the focus of leaders ought to be on functions, tasks and behaviours and that if these functions are carried out competently the work of others in the organisation will be facilitated. Most approaches to managerial leadership also assume that the behaviour of organisational members is largely rational. Authority and influence are allocated to formal positions in the organisational hierarchy.[6]

Although management was largely superseded by notions of leadership in the late 1990s in much of the literature,[7] governments in many countries, including the UK, have continued to advance their educational reform programmes through a managerial perspective, expecting schools to introduce and enforce external policy decisions through hierarchical methods.[8] Evidence of this can be seen in examples of some of the managerial functions:[9]

- **Supervision:** School leaders increasingly monitor the activities of classroom teachers through observations, book scrutiny and data drops.

- **Behaviour controls:** Classroom 'non-negotiables', prescribed teaching practices, excessive marking policies, and directed intervention for 'under-performing' students all reduce the autonomy of teachers in deciding where best to spend their time and effort.

- **Output controls:** Detailed statistical analysis of results, attribution of students' performance to teachers, performance related pay, student/class targets and assessment regimes which generate performance data against which progress is measured and teacher effectiveness is judged.

Recent research by Skinner et al[10] evidences the impact of this managerialist approach on teacher stress and wellbeing. Through in-depth, structured interviews with teachers who had experienced mental health problems, they explored the link between managerial actions and teacher stress, and its impact on identity. The work-related causes of the mental health problems experienced by teachers reflected earlier, quantitative studies which have identified factors such as organisational change, workload and lack of managerial support. However, the qualitative approach also highlighted conflict between what teachers were asked to do and their professional identity: uncertainty over what was now expected of them and loss of autonomy as a result of increasingly bureaucratic processes. In particular, the performance review process was a cause of significant stress as teachers' behaviours were made public, causing some to view their success (or failure) increasingly in relation to their colleagues, or with reference to what the headteacher would think of them.

Skinner et al describe how the managerialist approach to education can change teachers' perceptions of their expertise. The knowledge they hold becomes useful in proving their effectiveness and the success of the school, rather than for the pupils' learning. Alongside this 'exteriorisation' of professional expertise[11] comes a deterioration of relationships between teachers, replacing informal chats about pupils and their learning with formal evaluative discussions about performance: both of the pupils and the teacher. The conflict this causes for the teacher is described well in the conclusion to the paper:

The teachers' and head teachers' comments express the tension between two opposing forces, one being the old view of what it means to be a teacher – that is, commitment, service to the school and pupils' learning, ownership of expertise and knowledge – and the other being the new managerialist view of being a teacher – that is, accountability, performativity, meeting standards, and stepping up to the presentation of the school in a new corporate world.

We can track many managerialist practices back to the isomorphic pressures discussed previously and to the 1988 Education Reform Act which introduced performance management targets, more high-stakes assessments for pupils, self-evaluation and external inspection. The introduction of school 'league tables' in 1992 and the promotion of 'school choice' alongside a change in the funding model such that schools received more of their income according to the number of students they admitted, created a pseudo-market for schools which encouraged open competition in a geographical area.[12] More than ever before, schools had to 'look good' as much as 'be good', and this meant a positive Ofsted report and high position in the league tables.

It is no wonder that the pressures of accountability, attracting students and delivering government policy have resulted in school leaders becoming distracted by the abstract. Consider the difference between what it takes to *look* good and what it means to *be* good for schools today:

Look good	Be good
Achieve high results	Provide a rich and rounded education
Attract lots of students	Meet the needs of your local community
Achieve 'Outstanding'	Do your best, without killing people
Keep staff costs down	Make staff want to stay for the long term
Drive up standards	Help people develop
No excuses	Tolerate mistakes
Play it safe	Take risks
Audit trail	Know your school
Look for best practice	Do what works in your context
Be relentless	Have a life outside of school
Check up on people	Trust people

Spending time on *looking* good means wasting energy on the superficial. It is a distraction from *being* good.

School structures

I cannot write about managerialism without mentioning multi-academy trusts (MATs). MATs are an organisational structure whereby a number of schools are owned and managed as one legal entity. In the UK, they have formed through mergers of single academy trusts, which themselves are schools which have claimed independence from local authority control. I am not, for the record, against MATs, but at their worst, they do appear to magnify the forces which lead to abstraction and can be a distraction for school leaders from the task of running a school.

I will illustrate my argument with a couple of examples. Some MATs have a tendency to centralise school policy and particular functions. This can make economic sense and can help build a 'corporate identity' for the MAT (although I'm yet to work out why a corporate identity is needed). Let's take the example of policies relating to personnel issues, e.g. pay and working conditions. As the employer, it is logical, even legally necessary, to offer consistent contractual rights to all the employees in the organisation. Yet each school within the MAT is contextually different and a 'best fit' approach to policy may limit my ability as a school leader to set up the school in the optimal way. For example, the school I lead may suffer from particularly high staff turnover, perhaps due to the cost of living or the challenging behaviour of students. As the headteacher of such a school, I will want every instrument possible at my disposal to increase the length of time teachers stay. I may make it financially attractive to stay on for more than two years with a bonus, or I might invest heavily in professional development and create promotion opportunities. The point is that if we want leaders to be responsive to the particular problems they face, we must give them the maximum powers and tools to do so. Power should be distributed, not centralised.

A useful metaphor for the nuanced settings school leaders will have at their disposal is a graphic equaliser: the ones you used to get on 1980s home stereos. There was a trend at the time to produce hi-fi stereos with increasingly fine-tuned graphic equalisers, perhaps up to 20 sliding buttons, each adjusting the dominance of one part of the frequency spectrum. As a teenager, I would spend ages getting the settings just right: not too much bass, slightly higher treble. Everyone knew you shouldn't just push all the buttons up to maximum or down to minimum – it sounded awful. Getting the balance just right in a school environment is also important. Applying this metaphor to staff working patterns, for example, one school may need to employ firm controls on workload to break bad habits among staff who are doing tasks that will have little impact, while another may crack down on a minority of staff who opt out of directed activities, creating a culture of dissent. Getting the tone of school culture right will require school leaders to use the right levers at the right time to create the 'settings' that work best for their organisation. Removing the control over some of these settings will only serve to make school leaders less effective.

A second feature of some MATs is the tendency to adopt standardised performance metrics so that the strengths and weaknesses of each school can be monitored at a distance and comparisons made between schools. While metrics (e.g. staff absence levels, cost control, student numbers) can be captured and compared with ease, the collection of these will mean leaders pay particular attention to them and prioritise, making this data look good. Furthermore, when these metrics attempt to measure intangible aspects of schools, such as whether students are learning, the measuring process becomes incredibly intrusive. Schools might find that they are required to synchronise their curriculum, assessment methodology, assessment timings and reporting cycle across the MAT, for instance. Performance data is a proxy for success but, like the abstract models discussed in Chapter 4, often fails to capture accurately the reality of whether students are being well educated.

It is not the remit of this book to provide a full and balanced critique of MATs, or any other school ownership models, but suffice to say, school leaders have enough outside distractions, without systems within their organisation threatening to take their focus away from the pupils, the curriculum and the specific challenges they face on a daily basis. MATs don't necessarily do this, but it is a tendency to guard against.

Leading in distracting times

School leaders face multiple distractions and pressures to improve abstract measures of success, rather than the substance of education itself. It is all very well calling for headteachers to be 'brave', but brave heads often get hung out to dry. School leaders must somehow chart a course through these choppy waters, staying focused on the destination while feeding the beasts in the ocean's depths that threaten to overturn the ship.

Summary of chapter substance

▬▬▬▬▬▬▬▬ **Substance (stuff)** What do we need to know?	There are forces which distract school leaders from doing the right thing for children, staff and their communities. Leaders are encouraged to think in abstract terms about what success looks like and can be caught up in pursuing superficial goals. This can be damaging for staff wellbeing and the quality of education provided.
▬▬▬▬▬▬▬ **Substance (significance)** Why is this important?	By recognising the forces that act upon them, leaders are more likely to prioritise being good over looking good.
▬▬▬▬▬▬ **Substance (validity)** How do we know it to be true?	The rising number of teachers leaving the profession and the documented cases of mental health problems arising from high-stakes accountability cultures both point to an unsustainable approach to educational leadership.

Further reading

For a full analysis of institutional isomorphism and the audit culture in schools, see: Allen, R. and Sims, S. (2018) *The Teacher Gap*. Abingdon: Routledge.

References

1. Harris, D. and Gilbert, I. (2013) *Brave Heads: How to Lead a School Without Selling Your Soul*. Carmarthen, Wales: Independent Thinking Press.

2. Hattie, J. (2012) *Visible Learning for Teachers*. Abingdon: Routledge.

3. Didau, D. (2015) *What if Everything You Knew About Education was Wrong?* Carmarthen, Wales: Crown House Publishing.

4. A transcript of Dr Rebecca Allen's lecture can be found here: www.bit.ly/2IvwBuB

5. DiMaggio, P. J. and Powell, W. W. (1983) 'The Iron Cage Revisited: Institutional Isomorphism and Collective Rationality in Organizational Fields', *American Sociological Review* 48 (2) pp. 147-160

6. Leithwood, K., Jantzi, D. and Steinbach, R. (1999) *Changing Leadership for Changing Times*. Buckingham: Open University Press.

7. Bush, T. and Glover, D. (2003) *School Leadership: Concepts and Evidence*. Nottingham: National College for School and Leadership.

8. Levacic, R., Glover, D., Bennett, N. and Crawford, M. (1999) 'Modern Headship for the Rationally Managed School: Cerebral and Insightful Approaches', *Education Management: Refining Theory*, Policy and Practice. London: Paul Chapman.

9. Myers, E. and Murphy, J. (1995), 'Suburban Secondary School Principals' Perceptions of Administrative Control in Schools', *Journal of Educational Administration* 33 (3) pp. 14-37.

10. Skinner, B., Leavey, G. and Rothi, D. (2019), 'Managerialism and Teacher Professional Identity: Impact on Well-being Among Teachers in the UK', *Educational Review* 1 (16).

11. Ball, S. J. (2003) 'The Teacher's Soul and the Terrors of Performativity', *Journal of Education Policy* 18 (2) pp. 215-228.

12. Leckie, G. and Goldstein, H. (2016) 'The evolution of school league tables in England 1992-2016: "Contextual value-added", "expected progress" and "progress 8"', *British Educational Research Journal* 43 (2) pp. 193-212.

Chapter 7
Curricular genericism

Bog standard genericism

My first foray into senior leadership in a school came on the back of the specialist schools' movement which Tony Blair introduced as a way of combatting the 'bog standard comprehensive'. I was appointed to lead the business and enterprise specialism at a boys' school in a leafy part of the south east of England. It was a great job, offering experience of senior leadership alongside considerable autonomy in driving a strategic priority for the school, which had the potential to change the school culture, curriculum and reputation. I threw myself head-first into the challenge, despite the resistance of a number of teachers who felt that the whole thing was a capitalist conspiracy, or progressive hogwash, or both. I think they had a point. As I said in the introduction: listen to the teacher-curmudgeon.

'Enterprise learning' became the vogue, featuring as part of the government's work-related learning strategy, and I busily set about creating a 'capability framework', guidance materials and even a software platform to capture the outcomes of students' enterprising endeavours. The school gained a national reputation for our work in this area and I was invited to share our approach at conferences across England. Enterprise learning, I claimed, not only prepared students for their future personal and working lives, but also provided a way of engaging students in the curriculum by allowing them to exercise creativity, solve problems and work in teams.

All of this seemed eminently reasonable at the time. But then, so did Thinking Hats, Bloom's taxonomy, Gardner's Multiple Intelligences, 21st Century skills and PLTS (the Personal, Learning and Thinking Skills embedded in the National Curriculum of the day). Progressivism dominated educational discourse and the legacy of this lives on in the generic leadership practices in today's schools.

Domain-free learning

Enterprise capabilities are but one example of the 'hollow skills' discussed in Chapter 2, predicated on the idea that skills can be transferred easily between domains of knowledge. Other examples include stand-alone critical thinking courses, literacy intervention and employability skills. In each case, there is an attempt to teach transferable skills separately to the subject disciplines across which they are to be applied. But even within subjects, notions of transferable skills exist, as evidenced by the National Curriculum (NC) levels which formed the basis of much of the assessment practice in schools for Key Stages 1 to 3, from 1988 all the way through to 2014, when they were unceremoniously pulled by the education secretary, Michael Gove. History teachers would instruct students in how to learn the skill of 'evaluating historical sources' and, in English, students were taught to 'make inferences', as if, once mastered, they would move between Ancient Rome and the Second World War, or between *To Kill a Mockingbird* and *Hamlet*, interpreting and inferring equally competently across eras and texts. Curricular genericism, meaning an abstraction from the domain-specific knowledge which forms the substance of subject disciplines, went largely unquestioned by all but a minority, who were side-lined as holding unorthodox, outdated views.

Infectious genericism

Throughout the 1990s, curricular genericism spread into other aspects of schooling, fuelled by Ofsted's progressive ideology and accountability pressures. Students' learning became defined as the distance travelled over time between two different snapshots of attainment (e.g. KS2 tests and GCSE grades), and – in between these points – as the progression in skills as students climbed the NC levels' ladder. Schools developed increasingly 'sophisticated' data systems to measure this progress, using this to hold to account both the students and their teachers, made possible by more powerful management information systems (and very colourful spreadsheets). The fact that the before and after tests and the conception of progress in between these points had no internal logic or consistency went unremarked upon as the illusion of progress, and the industry it created, fed the narrative of able students achieving success and the less able, or disadvantaged, destined to achieve a lower outcome on the 'flight path'. Pedagogy also caught the genericism bug, as three-part lessons, plenaries and methods to 'engage' students became de rigour: an 'intransitive pedagogy'[1] in which the teaching process sits separate from the object of study. Under pressure to prove that students were making progress, schools innovated new approaches to marking, encouraged by the 'good practice' highlighted by Ofsted reports, the success of which was judged on how universally teachers across subject disciplines adopted the latest, dialectic approach. Graded lesson observations followed, based on the belief that good teaching could be seen in the generic techniques used by teachers and the progression of skills observable in children's exercise books. Sitting above all these generic practices loured the 'performance management system': its targets based on generic data; its judgements based on generic observations and book scrutiny; its professional development, which instructed teachers in pedagogies divorced from the substance of the subject to be taught. Genericism raged like a virulent disease.

Leadership hosts

School leaders were not the source of the genericism disease but they became its host, often not suffering the symptoms, but spreading the virus across their schools. Senior leadership posts were invented to oversee the new genericism: data manager, pupil progress co-ordinator, raising attainment lead, AHT for teaching standards, intervention co-ordinator, senior leader in charge of self-evaluation. Leadership genericism proliferated as 'one size fits all' systems excused leaders from the far more intellectually challenging task of understanding the distinct curricular and pedagogical traditions of the subject disciplines. A generation of senior leaders, knowing nothing other than this genericism as they rose through the ranks of management, each held to account through abstract and generalised measures of their success, took control of our schools and struggled to imagine another way to lead.

Progressive ideology based on a misunderstanding of how humans learn, combined with the isomorphic pressures described in the last chapter and the consequent rise in managerialism created a conception of expert leadership as something which sits separately from the curricular disciplines. Expert leadership became the skill with which leaders implemented their plans, held others to account, designed systems, monitored student progress and drove school improvement. Generic leaders were the ideal solution to lead generic schools.

The demise of curricular genericism?

In January of 2017, Amanda Spielman commenced her role as Her Majesty's Chief Inspector of Education. In her inaugural speech at the 2017 ASCL Conference,[2] she spoke of her concern about the effect that performance tables were having on schools and how accountability measures were leading some to narrow the curriculum for students. She set out her intent to make the curriculum a more central focus to Ofsted inspections and commissioned 'in-depth research into the curriculum'.

Fast-forward to January 2019: Spielman launched a consultation into a new Education Inspection Framework (EIF) at the Sixth Form Colleges Association Winter Conference,[3] in which she stated:

> The title is the headline: it's all about the substance of education, and how that is examined at inspection... we have collectively realised in recent years how easy it can be for practitioners and institutions, and indeed for policy makers and inspectorates, to lose sight of the substance amid the noise.

This was not the first time Spielman had used the word 'substance', but this speech signalled that the term would be at the heart of the EIF. She continued:

> So what do we understand to be the real substance of education? What is its core purpose, and what is Ofsted's role? At the very

heart of education sits the vast accumulated wealth of human knowledge and what we choose to impart to the next generation. I have made no secret of the fact that I think that curriculum, the 'what is taught and why', has had too small a share of inspection consideration for many years, and that this has contributed to the gradual erosion of curriculum thinking in early years, schools and post-16. This draft framework is built around a rebalanced set of judgements that restore curriculum to its proper place as one of the main considerations in good education. And in turn, I hope, to the forefront of educators' minds.

Spielman's explicit focus on 'what is taught and why' signalled a profound shift for Ofsted, away from genericism and towards curricular substance. In the consultation documentation that followed, the phrase 'the curriculum *is* the progression model' appeared again and again: an absolute rejection of data-driven progress models in favour of evidence of what knowledge and skills students had specifically acquired. Despite claims that Ofsted had no preferred curriculum model, the message to schools was clear. No more flight paths; no more curriculum narrowing; no more 'soft' subjects. We want to know what students know, and that this knowledge is powerful and secure.

Cognitive science and the new traditionalism

But Ofsted were not first to the party. A growing movement of research-informed educationalists, fuelled by developments in cognitive science, given a voice through social media and brought together by organisations such as ResearchED, were reigniting what might be called a 'traditionalist' view of schooling (although the name appears to stick in the throat of many given the label).

As with any emerging community online, diverse views and conflicting opinions are exchanged. However, broad consensus[4] has emerged around the most reliable findings of cognitive science, including the belief that:

- Children connect new knowledge to existing knowledge, and in doing so construct a mental schema of a domain of knowledge.

- We have limited space in our working memory to hold information, so it is easy to overload children with new information.

- All subjects have facts which, if committed to long-term memory, ease the strain on working memory when children are solving problems.

- New knowledge will be forgotten unless it is periodically retrieved from long-term memory. Retrieval practice is one of the most powerful ways of learning.

- Transferring knowledge and skills to a novel problem requires knowledge of the problem's context and a deep understanding of a problem's underlying structure.

- To understand a problem's underlying structure, it is necessary to consider a range of concrete examples and relate these to abstract representations.

- Explicit instruction by teachers will be more effective than approaches which leave students to construct their own knowledge, as the former will provide the necessary conditions to accommodate the learning process described above.

The findings of cognitive science appear to be contradictory to many of the generic pedagogic ideas which have been dominant in English schools, including the notion of transferable skills, skills-ladders, linear progress models, group work, three-part lessons and 'higher order' skills. Instead, this field of research moves us towards an explicit focus on knowledge construction through instructional methods: to the 'substance' of the curriculum.

Disciplinary distinctiveness

Cognitive science offers us a way out of the grip of the progressive genericism of the recent past. However, we must be cautious not to replace one broad-brush approach with another by applying our understanding of how we learn to the curriculum without regard for the distinct disciplinary traditions and features of subject domains. In a blog post entitled *Genericism's Children*,[1] Christine Counsell describes what she sees as a crisis in our conceptions of senior curriculum leadership:

Such a crisis is characterized by an absence of curricular reflection on differing knowledge structures and their epistemic power, on the place of knowledge in definitions of progress, on subjects as distinctive yet shifting traditions into which pupils can be inducted, on the interplay of layers and forms of knowledge within subjects, and on knowledge as the inclusion issue: what Hirst and Peters called 'public modes of knowledge' and the access they give us to educated conversation.

Counsell highlights a tension between the disciplinary reasoning of the subject specialist and the generic approach to pedagogy adopted by many schools. This tension is played out as senior leaders concern themselves with how the curriculum is taught (teaching and learning) and *how well* (progress, assessment, data, outcomes), while paying little regard to *what* is being learned, thereby creating an 'intransitive pedagogy' – pedagogy without an object.

One example of intransitive pedagogy is the practice of asking teachers to structure their lessons around Bloom's Taxonomy[5] which results in generic conceptions of terms like 'analyse' and 'evaluate'. These terms mean very different things in different disciplines, or even between one specific domain of knowledge and another. What is it we seek to analyse? What specific knowledge do we require? What is its status? What role does each element play and how do these items of knowledge relate to each other? Michael Fordham describes words such as 'analyse' as needing an object – what Orwell called 'pretentious diction'.[6] By employing generalised language, we lose an understanding of the difference, the particular, the nuance, the substance. Fordham argues that it is easier to ignore the differences as these create 'noise' and 'contradictions'; differences are inconvenient for those attempting to lead the curriculum.[7] However, in generalising, we risk sacrificing the 'complexity and richness' of our curriculum at the altar of management convenience.

What is so important about the case for disciplinary distinctiveness made by Counsell, Fordham and others is that it transcends notions of 'progressive' and 'traditional' ideology, both of which may be caught in the trap of genericism. Progressivism has us teaching '21st century skills', checking progress through 'mini-plenaries' and breaking down subject boundaries. Neo-traditionalism, drawing on cognitive science, provides generalisations for how students acquire knowledge, encourages regular retrieval, and advises us to 'chunk' knowledge to help working memory. In both approaches, there is little discussion, as yet, of the objects of learning and how the nature of the knowledge within each subject discipline may determine the pedagogy, rather than a generalised pedagogic understanding being applied across subject disciplines. As Fordham states:

> The overarching orthodoxy at the moment... is that our starting point ought to be generic ideas (such as 'learning', 'pupil outcomes', etc.) with these ideas then considered in the context of particular subjects. My argument would be that this is back to front: the thing which is being taught ought to have primacy.[6]

How will school leadership adapt?

It would appear that there is a pincer movement around school leaders, manoeuvring them away from the old orthodoxy and towards something new. Official organisations (like Ofsted, the Education Endowment Foundation and the DfE) on the one side are exerting coercive isomorphic pressures on schools to adopt evidence-informed and curriculum-focused models of school improvement. Groundswell, informal networks (gaining traction through the blogs and social media) on the other side are exerting peer pressure to achieve similar objectives. Each side is entwined through an internet embrace, with figureheads of the establishment like Ofsted's National Director, Sean Harford, actively engaging through Twitter with the bloggers and agitators.

Whatever your views on these developments, we can all recognise the winds of change which are blowing through the school system and no doubt will empathise with the school leaders once again asked to question everything they thought they knew. Once comfortable in their curricular genericism, there is the sense that everything is about to change. The shift from curricular genericism to curriculum substance will require us to radically rethink what senior curriculum leadership means. As Counsell notes, you cannot expect senior leaders to be an expert in every subject, but we should expect our school leaders to be more attentive to creating the conditions in which subject experts thrive.[5]

Critical to the success of the new orthodoxy will be the extent to which school leaders are coerced to adapt rather than transform their practice willingly. The recent history of educational reform in England suggests that coercion will be a significant factor, with school leaders required to be the instrument of government in enacting change. Unless school leaders fully understand and accept the rejection of curricular genericism and intellectually subscribe to the new paradigm being presented to them, transformation efforts will be superficial and poorly received by the profession. For example, leaders may attempt to pay lip-service to Ofsted expectations by producing documentation and audit trails which 'demonstrate' their curriculum intent, implementation and impact. New processes might be overlaid onto the old, with the result that teachers are expected to adopt additional practices, rather than set aside the old in favour of the new.

But an element of coercion is probably required as the binds to curricular genericism will be hard to break. School leaders' identities are often conceived of (by themselves and others) in generic ways. School leadership is regarded as a separate domain of knowledge within the school system: as something distinct which you can gain expertise in, somehow separate to the curriculum, which is the object of the school's activities. When teachers become leaders, we imagine that they enter a secret garden of knowledge, leaving behind their subject domain and turning their attention to the task of overseeing – cultivating the ability to make sense of the whole organisation through generalisations. To challenge the idea of leadership expertise as something separate from the curriculum is threatening, as it suggests that much of the 'expertise' actually resides with the teacher, not the leader, and that the role of the leader is to respect, seek to understand and to enable this expertise to flourish. This is the forgotten aspect of leadership expertise: to cultivate the specific, not the general. Altering our perspective on where expertise lies within a school is a radical shift which may feel undermining to the leader's authority and disruptive to the organisational hierarchy. In a sense, it turns the organisation upside-down, moving the locus of control to those at the battlefront and away from the generals (and the 'generals'). This conception of leadership positions senior leaders as servile to the curriculum and as needing to be sensitive to the knowledge of the expert.

It feels a world away from the hierarchical, accountability-driven leadership model which is dominant across much of the educational system today.

To gain a sense of how disruptive to leaders' self-identity a rejection of curricular genericism might be, consider the beliefs which arise from genericism, but which would be fundamentally questioned, perhaps even overturned, by its deconstruction:

- I can tell a good lesson when I see it.
- Scrutinising children's work helps me see if they are making progress.
- Equipping teachers with the techniques and skills they need will improve their teaching.
- Progress data enables me to see which students are falling behind.
- I can set targets for student attainment at GCSE based on their prior attainment and identify if they are on track to achieve this.
- Intervention strategies should be targeted at those whose grades fall below expectation.
- We have a cross-curricular strategy to improve resilience and build skills for life.
- Our new independent learning lessons will give the students the confidence and toolkit to rely less on the teacher.
- We teach transferable skills which students apply with increasing sophistication as they encounter new topics.
- We use GCSE assessment criteria all the way back to Year 7 to chart a pathway along which students will progress.
- Our CPD offer is focused on pedagogies which all subjects can employ to raise standards of teaching and learning.

These examples illustrate how embedded curricular genericism is in schools as the language feels familiar to our ears and will have rolled off the tongues of most school leaders in recent times. What language will replace this? How should we talk about school leadership if we genuinely recognise the central importance of subject domains? A new language is required.

Along with beliefs, the day-to-day activities carried out by leaders will also change if a new orthodoxy takes hold. What school leaders talk about, what they look for and what decisions they make (or allow others to make) will change. When in a lesson, leaders may look less at the activities the teacher and students are engaged in and more at what is being taught and how the 'object' of the lesson affects the dynamic. More time might be spent asking teachers how they are creating a curriculum narrative for students and how they know if students are progressing in relation to this. Rather than spending time designing and managing data tracking and intervention systems, leaders may want to ensure that teachers' knowledge of their students' learning is sound and that they take immediate action to adjust their teaching when students appear to struggle with the curriculum content. These shifts are more like an earthquake than a tremor, as a move away from curricular genericism has the power to transform the landscape of schools.

Undoubtedly, from the wreckage, some generic curriculum leadership approaches will remain, and so they should. Standardisation serves a purpose when it allows leaders to filter out the noise and identify patterns which inform management understanding and decision-making. However, common processes should not compromise the disciplinary differences between subjects[8] or detract from the curriculum. It is often said that schools are people organisations. It is indeed important to remember that it is people that make schools what they are and leaders forget this at their peril. However, I would argue that schools are, first and foremost, knowledge organisations. It is the intellectual capital of the adults, and how this is transmitted to the children such that they are enabled to access powerful knowledge to help them live fulfilling lives should remain the central focus of school leaders. When school leaders lose sight of disciplinary knowledge and place leadership expertise over subject expertise, we create an educational orthodoxy without substance.

Summary of chapter substance

▰▰▰▰▰▰ **Substance (stuff)** What do we need to know?	Subject disciplines have been largely overlooked in recent decades in favour of curricular genericism. This is changing, as influential organisations (such as Ofsted) and informal networks are exerting pressure on schools to elevate the status of disciplinary knowledge.
▰▰▰▰▰ **Substance (significance)** Why is this important?	School leadership has been instrumental in the spread of curricular genericism and has itself fallen foul of overly generic approaches which, at worst, undermine the efforts of subject experts to engage students in their disciplines. As the orthodoxy shifts, school leaders will need a new conception of their purpose and practice. This change is likely to be painful, but potentially transformative.
▰▰▰▰▰ **Substance (validity)** How do we know it to be true?	The paradigm shift can be seen in grass-roots movements such as ResearchED, in learning communities on social media, and now in national policy by agencies such as Ofsted and the DfE. However, it is uncertain as to how these changes will play out and whether they will result in a positive outcome for our children and schools.

Further reading

Young, M. and Lambert, D. (2014) *Knowledge and the Future School*. London: Bloomsbury.

References

1. Counsell, C. (2016) 'Genericism's children', *The dignity of the thing* [Online], 11 January. Retrieved from: www.bit.ly/337CDJQ

2. Amanda Spielman's inaugural speech at the 2017 ASCL conference can be found here: www.bit.ly/2AR9aHU

3. Amanda Spielman's speech at the Sixth Form Colleges Association Winter Conference 2019 can be found here: www.bit.ly/2ANzRxE

4. For a digestible summary of the findings of cognitive science, see *The Learning Scientists* website: www.bit.ly/2wNJokD

5. Counsell, C. (2018) 'In Search of Senior Curriculum Leadership: Introduction – A Dangerous Absence', *The dignity of the thing* [Online], 27 March. Retrieved from: www.bit.ly/30UsTRH

6. Fordham, M. (2015) 'Edu-babble: The Language of the Generic', *Clio et cetera* [Online], 7 January. Retrieved from: www.bit.ly/2ViW9jK

7. Fordham, M. (2018) 'The Scourge of Curriculum: Genericism's Destructive Power', *Clio et cetera* [Online], 15 April. Retrieved from: www.bit.ly/2nnaSO8

8. Woodcock, J. (2018) 'The Importance of Being Particular', *Trying to make sense* [Online], 27 April. Retrieved from: www.bit.ly/2oVYCVk

Chapter 8
Leaving genericism behind

In the introduction to this book, I asked you to imagine a pair of spectacles which, when worn, would bring into focus the 'substance' of school leadership by filtering out the abstract theories, distractions, ideology and management flannel which too often blur our vision. In Section 1 I have described some of the things that have clouded our view of leadership and contributed to leaders in schools prioritising the generic over the specific. Before we turn our attention fully to matters of substance, it is worth summarising the ways in which school leaders are pulled towards the generic, lest we be drawn in that direction again.

Salvaging from the leader-ship

In Chapter 1, I argued that, despite many years of theorising and research, we have failed to reach a consensus on what leadership is, or even come close to doing so. The absence of an agreed definition of leadership means it is a loose and ever-changing theoretical construct, and as such is not a good subject for research or a reliable guide for practitioners. Many of the attempts to describe effective leadership rely on generalisations, broad descriptors of leadership 'qualities' and unverifiable causal relationships. The context within which the leader operates is frequently brushed over or devalued in an attempt to make generalisable claims, and in doing so undervalues the 'object' of leadership: a lack of concern for *what* it is that is being led.

In Chapter 4, I suggest that we may be wasting our time searching for an elusive 'theory of everything' to explain leadership, and should perhaps be content with a verifiable 'theory of something' which points towards how we should carry out specific aspects of our roles as school leaders. And even then, while theoretical models are useful in helping us work out where we are going and, broadly, the path to take, we won't really know the challenge we are facing until we actually walk the terrain ourselves. The devil, as they say, is in the detail, but it is also in the context within which we work. The 'strong claims' made about leadership are supported by evidence, to varying degrees, but even the most well-supported theories for what effective leaders do will not necessarily help us improve our own leadership. When we attempt to mimic the models of 'great leaders' presented to us, we risk losing sight of the reality of the challenges in our particular school. We should beware of leadership mythology and define for ourselves what success looks like in our context.

I do not dismiss all leadership theory out of hand, but we must proceed with caution. There are some truths hidden among the abstract theories and management flannel – like nuggets of gold mixed up in the sand – but we must beware of fool's gold, also.

Expert leadership

The notion of leadership as being separate and distinct from the concrete reality of what is being led was critiqued further in Chapters 2 and 3 in relation to the dangers of ignoring domain-specific knowledge. Particularly troublesome is the idea of generic leadership skills which, it is claimed by some, can be acquired and applied by leaders across contexts and domains. While generic skills do exist, they are acquired through, and are useful in, our daily lives but play a limited role in the complex and highly technical task of leading a school. Becoming an expert leader requires extensive domain-knowledge and procedural fluency in the application of this knowledge to solving complex problems. A failure to grasp this leaves us susceptible to overestimating our own competence, wasting valuable effort in developing 'leadership skills' and neglecting to equip ourselves with the knowledge we need to make good decisions.

Further support for the importance of domain-specific knowledge comes from the field of intelligence research. We find that we want our leaders to be intelligent, and that it is generally advantageous for them to be so. However, many aspects of intelligence appear to be fixed, with an exception to this being the quantity and quality of what we know. Knowing more appears to be a good route to becoming cleverer. But what we need in our leaders is not general intelligence but domain-specific intelligence: we want our leaders to be knowledgeable in the right way. Domain-specific knowledge, the 'dark matter' of adult intelligence, has arguably been underestimated in our concept of intelligence; particularly in relation to occupational expertise.

We should be sceptical of those who claim to have mastered the skills of leadership and reject conceptions that pay little attention to the role that domain-specific knowledge plays.

Distracting times

In Chapters 5 and 6, I described the social and political environment which has pulled the education system towards genericism over the last 20 years. Superficial measures of success have dominated the thoughts of school leaders, whereby exam results and Ofsted labels have become the goal rather than the indicator of educational quality. Isomorphic pressures and unprincipled management practices have spread destructive practices across the system. Leadership has often become managerial and controlling due to demand for rapid improvement and implied threat over the consequences of complacency. I argue that it has become increasingly difficult to stay focused on the needs of the school's community during this era, and to avoid distraction and the pursuit of looking good over being good. Teachers have also been distracted by an audit culture which demands that they are not only competent, but can prove that they are. The consequences are a teacher shortage and workload crisis.

During this period, we have created a leadership fetish, idolising 'heroic' leaders and, in doing so, creating an expectation of school leaders which few feel able to live up to. But the school turnaround efforts have too often been pseudo-transformational; driven without principles or regard to the sustainability of school improvement.

The challenge for school leadership in the next decade will be to steer a path of integrity through our muddled system, taking our share of the blame and playing a more central role in system improvement.

Genericism at the heart of schools

In Chapter 7, I reflected on the progressive ideology which has dominated discourse about the curriculum and the purpose of schools since the end of the last century. I cast school leaders as being hosts for the distribution of curricular genericism, spreading the contagion through pedagogic ideas, data systems, self-evaluation processes, monitoring activities and performance management. In this era, a false concept of leadership expertise in schools has taken hold, whereby leaders specialise in the generic and deliberately abstract themselves from the substance of the curriculum. There are signs that curricular genericism is coming to an end but dismantling the structures which support this orthodoxy will be difficult. School leaders may be the source of greatest resistance to change, as they will be required to lead in different ways and reconsider what it means to be an expert: to learn to cultivate the specific, not the general. It is far from clear whether the new orthodoxy will be perceived as empowering or another unwelcome coercive pressure on schools to, once again, adapt.

It is no wonder that school leadership seems so difficult and bewildering to many of those brave enough to try it. Reliable guidance and evidence for what works is notable by its absence, yet we are expected to transform our schools with heroic effort and skill while we are pulled in different directions by ideological and political forces. If this analysis of the recent history and state of our education system seems a little bleak, I apologise. However, I do think we have got ourselves into a bit of a pickle.

But I offer you hope and some practical ways to move forward. It is time to put on the glasses which will filter out that which we wish to ignore, and focus sharply on matters of substance. As I stated in the Introduction, for our purposes, we take 'substance' to mean:

Substance: the matter of which the thing consists.

What do leaders actually need to know?

How is this knowledge developed into expertise?

Substance: the most important or essential part of something.

Where should school leaders focus their attention?

What will make the most difference to the children in our schools?

Substance: a meaningful and valid point ('the argument has substance').

What do we know to be true about leadership?

What evidence do we have to support our claims?

We have already come across some ideas which will prove useful to us in our quest for leadership substance. Here they are again – pack them in your travel bag to take with us.

The importance of knowledge

A central theme of this book is that school leadership requires extensive knowledge. I contend that effective leadership is founded on a deep knowledge of the technical, social and contextual. But it is not sufficient to merely know lots: leaders must set about developing fluency in the execution of their roles through repeated attempts to apply their knowledge to solve challenging problems. As we shall see, it is the specific things that leaders do which mark out their leadership; therefore, a focus on the particular, over the general, is of significant importance.

The concepts relevant to this theme are:

Domain-specific knowledge: knowledge which pertains to a particular field of enquiry or set of related problems.

Procedural fluency: more commonly known as 'skills', procedural fluency is acquired through the repeated practice of applying relevant, sophisticated domain-specific knowledge to real-world scenarios. These skills are connected to the domain of knowledge and are therefore not transferable to different domains.

Mental schema: the vast, interconnected web of knowledge constructed over time. School leaders will assimilate new knowledge into their mental model to 'make sense' of the challenges they face.

Expertise

If leadership effectiveness is rooted in domain-specific knowledge, then it follows that a leader's expertise is bound to specific functions and domains. Rather than think in terms of becoming an 'expert leader', we should aim to develop expertise in the leadership of particular domains (e.g. curriculum leadership), and in executing specific functions (e.g. improving assessment practice).

The concepts relevant to this theme are:

Domain-specific leadership expertise: a high level of proficiency in the leadership of a particular function or domain, such that the common problems encountered are resolved confidently and competently.

Heuristics: mental shortcuts employed to help make decisions quickly. School leaders will compare the surface features of problems to determine possible solutions but may lead to bias or unreliable solutions.

Domain-specific intelligence (ds): using occupationally-related knowledge to achieve a desired goal.

School context

An essential element of the knowledge school leaders require is an understanding of their school context. This theme will be explored more in the coming chapters to highlight how central contextual knowledge is to leaders in performing many behaviours associated with strong leadership, including communicating a vision, showing concern for others and solving problems.

The concepts relevant to this theme are:

Social relations: how members of the organisation relate, which is influenced by their personalities, personal history and how they are grouped.

Culture: the ways in which members of the school normally behave and expect things to be done.

The curriculum

An understanding of the curriculum is possibly the most important knowledge a school leader can possess. How we conceive of the curriculum will affect our expectations around teaching, assessment and student progress, and even determine how we perceive the purpose of schooling and our role as leaders. I have advocated that school leaders take the time to understand subject disciplines so that their leadership is mindful of disciplinary distinctiveness and enables knowledge to flourish.

The concepts relevant to this theme are:

Curriculum substance: an explicit focus on disciplinary knowledge and how it is selected and sequenced to construct a coherent curriculum.

Disciplinary distinctiveness: the features of a disciplinary domain which make it distinct from others.

Knowledge organisations: viewing schools from the perspective that knowledge is central to their purpose.

Leadership integrity

Leaders wield great power in schools. It is not sufficient for leaders to be highly knowledgeable and skilled; their decisions must be underpinned by moral purpose and be coherent with the values they hold true. A value which I hope runs throughout this book is integrity. Leaders with integrity will focus on the needs of students and resist pressures and distractions to do otherwise. Integrity means the pursuit of meaningful educational goals over superficial notions of success, placing others before oneself, and valuing human wellbeing over performance. Leaders with substance are principled and resolute.

And so we leave genericism behind and turn our attention to matters of substance. In the next section, we will explore what leadership with substance looks like, before turning our attention to how we might develop better leaders and bring matters of substance to the fore in our school system.

Section 2
The Substance of Leadership

Chapter 9
Expert leaders

In Section 1, I concluded that leadership must have an object, and therefore leaders must develop expertise in the domain in which they perform their role. In this chapter, I will consider the nature of this expertise and how it makes leaders more effective.

Complexity

Expertise only becomes necessary in complex situations which humans have encountered only recently in our evolution. Often, these situations are culturally constructed, such as those we come across in the workplace. Not all workplaces are complex, but those that require technical, specialised and multi-disciplinary knowledge will present unusual and difficult problems to overcome.

When we are faced with everyday problems, we solve them effortlessly by applying our biologically-primary[1] skillset and socially constructed knowledge. For example, if we find ourselves lost in a strange town, we will employ ingrained problem-solving strategies: we look for information which indicates where we are or the direction we need to go, or we ask people around us who might have the solution to our problem. We will also draw on the everyday knowledge we have acquired as a result of living in the society we live in. For example, we know that many town centres have maps placed in populated areas, signposts at key junctions and street names attached to a wall at the end of a block.

In schools, we come across problems for which our general knowledge and skills alone will not be sufficient. Schools present particularly complex and challenging problems because:

- The knowledge to be taught is often selected on the basis that it will not be acquired by students through their everyday experience in their family or society. We are not biologically primed to acquire this knowledge naturally (for example, learning to write or perform long division). The core activity of schools is therefore set up to be difficult for those involved.

- Children, upon whom the success of the educational process depends, are in a constant state of developmental change and do not possess intellectual maturity or psychological stability. Their responses are often unpredictable and inconsistent.

- There is considerable uncertainty around how the educational process should best be carried out, and success is difficult to quantify and measure.

- The purpose of schooling is contested and there are multiple, often competing, priorities and goals.

- Schools are subject to ideological, social, economic, cultural, technical, legal and political change and influence.

- There are multiple parties with vested interests, including parents, society, government, higher education and industry. Each party overestimates their understanding of the educational process as they were all once subject to an experience of schooling. Folk knowledge, myth and misunderstanding often take the place of evidence and expertise.

- The differences in the communities served by schools means there is no transferable model which will prove effective across all contexts, therefore 'good practice' will rarely be context independent. Innovation will either take place at the level of the individual school or involve significant reworking of new approaches tried elsewhere to make them palatable and effective in a different context. System-wide improvement is therefore evolutionary rather than planned and deliberate.

Schools are considered to be complex rather than complicated systems. Complicated systems have many components, but the system as a whole can be understood by examining its components and the ways in which they interact. A computer is a good example of a complicated system, as it comprises multiple, sophisticated components which interact to produce predictable outcomes. Similarly, schools have multiple, interacting components, but the relationships between these factors are not linear, and there is a significant element of randomness and unpredictability. Causal relationships in schools may be weak and subject to change, which means that schools are in a constant evolutionary state. The term 'CELLS' has been coined to describe such organisations, which stands for Complex, Evolving, Loosely-Linked Systems.[2] To understand the nature of the expertise required to lead a school, one must grasp the notion of complexity. For complicated systems, it is possible to come to know everything required to 'master' the domain, but expertise in a complex system means a constant quest for understanding: unlearning what was previously known to be true and coming to terms with the uncertain feeling of sands shifting beneath your feet.

To lead in a school is to grapple with complexity. Consider, for example, a decision about what to teach students concerning issues faced by LGBT individuals and communities. On the face of it, the task appears as simple as creating some PSHCE (Personal, Social, Health and Citizenship Education) resources and perhaps providing some training to staff asked to deliver these. However, we will need to start with an understanding of the recent Sex and Relationships Education Act and what it requires of schools. We will then begin to think through age-appropriateness of content, what prior knowledge students will have and where in the curriculum such matters may already be taught. Next, our thoughts may turn to the community the school serves: what might be the expectations, concerns and views of parents? What controversy exists in wider society and how have schools been portrayed in the media who have taken a strong, moral stance on LGBT issues? This one problem alone will require extensive technical, social and contextual knowledge; an ability to weigh up competing priorities to reach a values-based decision which could have significant repercussions for the school. Complex problems are encountered daily in schools and multiple solutions are possible in each case. Expertise is how we, as humans, overcome this complexity.

Problems

The word 'problem' arises frequently when we consider expertise. It is a word which comes with negative connotations in everyday use. We may ask 'what's your problem?' when someone appears to object to us, or present barriers to someone's suggestion by stating 'the problem with that is...'. However, I wish to use the term here in a way that is neutral: a 'problem', for our purposes, is a matter which requires the application of expertise. Defined in this way, we can consider school leadership as consisting of numerous problems, and the task of leadership as making decisions about how to proceed towards the desired goal. That is not to say that leadership is a state of persistently overcoming difficult hurdles (although some days it feels that way), rather that it is the continuous process of finding the best way forward to achieve a desirable outcome.

The problems encountered in schools might be straightforward but are more often fiendishly complex. The philosopher and sociologist Donald Schon differentiates using the analogy of the high, hard ground versus the swampy lowlands in his description of such problems.[3]

> In the varied topography of professional practice, there is a high, hard ground overlooking a swamp. On the high ground, manageable problems lend themselves to solutions through the use of research based theory and technique. In the swampy lowlands, problems are messy and confusing, and incapable of technical solution. The irony of this situation is that the problems of the high ground tend to be relatively unimportant to individuals or society at large, however great their technical interest may be, while in the swamp lie the problems of greatest human concern. The practitioner is confronted with a choice. Shall he remain on the high ground where he can solve relatively unimportant problems according to his standards of rigor, or shall he descend to the swamp of important problems where he cannot be rigorous in any way he knows how to describe.

Schon's conception of swampy problems connects to our understanding of schools as complex organisations. Viewed in this way, we begin to see that leadership expertise must consist of an ability to make sense of complexity, grapple with swampy problems and stay afloat psychologically in a sea of ambiguity.

Problems also have differing levels of granularity. We might have an overall problem of improving student behaviour across the school. However, breaking this down, we can consider the problem of changing the behaviours of staff when they respond to challenging students, the problem of how to administer sanctions, or the problem of creating a rewards system that is fairly applied. At a micro level, we might consider the nature of interactions between students and staff and the problems associated with de-escalating specific instances of conflict.

How do experts solve complex problems?

In Chapter 2, we touched upon the relationship between complex problems, domain-knowledge and expertise. Experts are able to solve complex problems by drawing on domain-specific knowledge and do so increasingly effortlessly. This process occurs fluidly, as the expert has knowledge of typical 'problem states'[4] along with the knowledge of how best one might proceed. For a school leader operating in a highly complex environment, they may require knowledge of tens of thousands of problem states in relation to a particular domain, at various levels of granularity. This knowledge will have been acquired through repeated exposure to 'similar' problems as, over time, the expert determines the underlying patterns and structures of problems, thereby becoming able to determine generalised 'problem states' against which the problem at hand can be compared.

As well as possessing a deep knowledge of problem states, experts also have procedural fluency in applying their domain-specific knowledge. Once they have determined the preferable solution to a given problem, they can skilfully execute the actions necessary to implement it. In this way, the expert knows what to do and how to do it.

The source of both hallmarks of the expert – procedural fluency and knowledge of problem states – is extensive, domain-specific knowledge held in long-term memory.[5] Furthermore, it is apparent that the greater the complexity of the problem, the more important domain-specific knowledge is.[6] We may therefore conclude that school leadership, given its immense complexity, requires the leader to possess a vast repertoire of relevant knowledge and that this is the key to their effectiveness.

These insights throw into question so much of the accepted wisdom about leadership. When we observe the visible features of highly effective leaders and marvel at the apparent ease with which they make rapid decisions, direct action and deliver improved outcomes, we attribute to the leader natural ability, exceptional skill and powerful charisma. We are longing to see genius, heroism, superhuman abilities and superior intelligence. What we do not see, or appreciate, as it is hidden in the mind, is the 'dark matter' of leadership: the extensive, domain-specific knowledge which has taken years of deliberate practice to acquire and refine. Expert leadership is neither flashy nor exceptional; it is grounded in a detailed knowledge of the context within which one leads, accessible to anyone who works to acquire it.

Is leadership transferable?

To what extent can we expect to move between contexts and be able to take our leadership expertise with us? If, today, we are a curriculum leader, and tomorrow we are asked to lead the pastoral team, will we need to start from scratch? What if we are a headteacher moving between schools, perhaps redeployed within a MAT to lead a troubled school? Most controversially, can we bring in leaders from another sector, such as health care, to take on the CEO position?

The good news is that there are some qualities we possess which will be transferable across contexts. Firstly, we can draw upon the biologically-primary knowledge which will enable us to assimilate into the new environment, orientate ourselves and form the relationships we will need to be successful. This knowledge includes the ability to listen and speak, engage in social relations and solve domain-general problems. Our understanding of intelligence, gained in Chapter 3, would also suggest that we will be able to employ our mental acuity, processing speed, attitudes and value-system to a new role. Therefore, when faced with novel problems, we should be able to think on our feet and weigh up options according to whether they fit with our beliefs as to what is worthwhile and morally defendable. Finally, we will have our personality, which we know to be correlated moderately with leadership effectiveness. Personality traits are often thought of as the 'big 5', namely:

- Openness to experience
- Conscientiousness
- Extroversion
- Agreeableness
- Neuroticism

Although the link between personality and leadership is not considered significant enough to be a reliable indicator of leadership potential,[7] possession of the first four of the above list seems likely to be a good fall-back for leaders finding themselves in a new context with little knowledge of the domain to rely on: willing to give it a go, hardworking, outwardly confident and concerned about their relations with other people.

None of the above constitute leadership expertise as it has been defined; however, in the absence of domain-specific knowledge, the characteristics identified will at least buy us time to develop the expertise we need and, in the meantime, win us enough allies to be able to draw on the expertise of others. Those of us who have taken on new leadership roles will no doubt recognise the feeling of flying by the seat of our pants while we work out what the hell we are meant to be doing.

Unfortunately, our hard-won domain-specific expertise will only be transferable to the extent that the contexts we are moving from and to have overlapping domains or similar problem states. Let's take the example of performing the same role but within two different schools; for example, a head of department role. It is likely that the technical knowledge required will be similar across the two posts. We would need a similar body of subject knowledge (to the extent that the curriculum is the same), of exam board requirements and external assessment processes. We might also find that we are faced with superficially similar problems: planning the curriculum, designing assessments or disciplining students. However, our knowledge of the social and cultural domain for our new school would be very limited and, as a result, the specific leadership problems encountered may appear similar, but the ways to solve these problems may be very different within the new context. What might have been effective in our last school may be far from ideal here. In such circumstances, we will find ourselves employing heuristics: rules of thumb arrived at by making superficial comparisons between the current problem and similar ones encountered in the past.

For more senior roles, such as a headteacher, a move between schools is likely to be even more challenging, as the knowledge of the school context will be an even more dominant aspect of the domain of knowledge needed. While an experienced headteacher will have developed extensive technical knowledge and a wide range of 'problem states' and heuristics to use as short-cuts to solve immediate problems, they will have to acquire a detailed understanding of the school community, culture and web of social connections. The wise headteacher will often sit back and observe for a period of time before making any significant changes in a school, for this reason.

Do school leaders need to be qualified teachers?

On the basis of the conclusions reached so far about the nature of leadership expertise, I would assert confidently that any school leader with responsibility for leading teachers should themselves have risen through the ranks and have considerable classroom experience. Teaching is no less complex and challenging than leading, and teachers have extensive domain-specific knowledge; much of which has been acquired through practice. This expertise must be part of the school leader's own domain of knowledge if they are to find solutions which have efficacy for teachers and students. This presents a significant challenge for school leaders for two reasons:

1. The greater their level of seniority, the less likely they are to continue to teach, therefore their expertise fades.

2. They will only have detailed curriculum knowledge in relation to the subjects they are qualified and/or experienced in teaching themselves.

It is difficult to quantify how much fading expertise, as a teacher, will impact on the effectiveness of school leadership. Some headteachers will proudly continue to teach and feel this gives them insight and credibility (I am firmly in this camp), while others will claim they do not have the time to teach and that it is a distraction from the role they are employed to do. The importance of continuing to teach might depend on the extent to which the leader's work directly relates to teaching and learning. For example, a headteacher may appoint others to lead on such matters and picture themselves overseeing, but not often directly influencing, the decisions made.

The second challenge, that of being restricted in your own subject expertise, may not appear to be a significant concern, at first glance. However, as we shall see in the next chapter, a failure to understand the differences between subject disciplines might significantly limit leadership effectiveness.

Expert leadership and organisational performance

There is a growing body of research into expert leadership and the effect it has on the performance of organisations. A paper by Amanda Goodall and Agnes Baker titled *A Theory Exploring How Expert Leaders Influence Performance in Knowledge-Intensive Organizations*,[8] provides a useful summary of the research and a discussion of the possible ways that expertise may make leaders more effective. The authors suggest that leaders in organisations which are primarily concerned with knowledge and intellectual capital should have a deep knowledge of the core business of their organisation. Such 'expert knowledge' has two components: industry experience and expert ability in the core business activity. Their analysis of the research in this field leads the authors to assert that expert knowledge should be the primary consideration for hiring panels appointing organisational leaders, and that other attributes such as leadership style and personality should come second to this.

Expert knowledge is defined by Goodall and Baker in a similar way to the explanation of expertise given earlier in this chapter, despite the latter deriving from the field of cognitive science and the former from management literature.

Experts differ from non-experts in a number of ways: knowledge is represented and bundled differently, they tend to think more holistically about problems (Bradley, Paul & Seeman, 2006),[9] and experts are more likely than novices to use abstract concepts to solve problems (Sembugamoorthy & Chandresekaren, 1986)[10]... Expert knowledge is acquired through a combination of technical education, domain-specific knowledge, practice and experience (Chase & Simon, 1973; de Groot, 1978)[11, 12]; it combines explicit and tacit knowledge (Nonaka & Takeuchi, 1995)[13] and it might also be thought of as a deep understanding that aids intuitive decision making, akin to wisdom (Tichy & Bennis, 2007).[14]

'Expertise-based intuition'[15] is where cognitive science and expertise research meet, and is the name given to the fluid decision-making process employed by expert leaders which is a key factor in high levels of performance. We previously came across this concept in our discussion of procedural fluency and 'problem states', which we identified as the cognitive source of expert leadership.

Leaders who have expertise in the domain in which they lead have a range of positive effects on their organisations. For example, evidence suggests that the technical competence of leaders is the most significant factor in the wellbeing of employees.[16] It appears that workers are happier if their immediate line manager could, if required, step in and do their job. Their ability to do so is greater if, for example, they have come up through the ranks in the company and possess significant technical knowledge relating to the core business of the organisation. Across different industrial contexts, in a range of countries within which the research took place, job satisfaction is higher if workers are led by people with expertise in the core activity of the business.

There is also evidence, from a range of industrial settings, that productivity is higher where the leaders have the technical expertise required to perform the jobs of those they are leading. For example, 'hospitals may do better if led by doctors rather than by general managers, U.S basketball teams do better when led by former All Star basketball players, Formula One racing teams do better if led by successful former racing drivers, and that universities do better when led by top researchers rather than talented administrators'.[17]

Research into the importance of technical competence for leaders has not extended into education. However, given what we know about the role of domain-specific knowledge in leadership, we might reasonably expect similar correlations to be found. It seems likely that those who lead schools need to possess expertise in teaching, and that maintaining this expertise is essential to staff wellbeing and productivity. Teachers rightly expect school leaders to know what they are talking about when it comes to the core business of the school. Indeed, the direct involvement of leaders in curriculum planning and professional development is associated with moderate to large leadership effects, suggesting that 'the closer leaders are to the core business of teaching and learning, the more likely they are to make a difference to students'.[18]

As yet, the causal relationship between expert leadership and benefits to organisations has not been fully explained. However, in the area of the 'creative industries', there is evidence to suggest that creative people perform better when they are led by those who share their competencies, as:[19]

- Evaluation of the work of people in these industries is more effectively carried out by those with expertise, and;
- Expert leaders are able to communicate more clearly with their employees, and;
- Expert leaders better articulate the needs and goals of the organisation.

Goodall and Baker draw together the research in the field of expert leadership to suggest how expert knowledge possessed by leaders may positively impact on the organisation. Firstly, they suggest that expert leaders make better decisions, which lead to better actions. Secondly, they argue that expertise is a signal to others that the leader is competent and trustworthy. It is worth outlining these claims a little, as they are pertinent to later chapters.

Proposition 1: Expert leaders make better decisions

Leaders who possess expert knowledge are more likely to make strategic decisions which are in the interest of the organisation as they are intrinsically motivated by the core business of the organisation and their interests align. They are prone to take the long view as they are inclined towards creating the right conditions for expertise to flourish, rather than achieving short-term goals to satisfy external agents.

Expert leaders understand the culture and value system of core workers and what motivates them to perform well, therefore will work to create the right conditions for job satisfaction and productivity. Expert leaders in complex organisations will be more able to live with ambiguity and resist implementing cumbersome accountability systems which oversimplify the job of core workers. They will set appropriate and realistic goals, be able to judge employee performance more reliably and have credibility in feeding back on how to improve.

Lastly, expert leaders will make better hiring decisions as they will recognise the characteristics which will lead to high performance.

Proposition 2: Expertise acts as a signal

Expert leaders are more credible than manager (non-expert) leaders and therefore command more respect and the co-operation of their followers. Credibility will mean expert leaders have influence as well as power. However, this credibility can be eroded if the leader does not perform well.

Credibility (particularly where it is maintained) may also signal to potential employees that the organisation is a desirable place to work. Hiring an expert leader may also indicate to other stakeholders the intentions of the organisation, casting it in a favourable light.

In combination, Goodall and Baker suggest that the expert leadership will result in improved organisational performance due to improved strategic decisions and greater employee performance in the long run. However, there are possible risks, as expert leaders may come with a narrow perspective (having worked within the same industry or organisation for many years), disciplinary bias (according to the particular specialism they held) and be institutionalised into the norms of the industry.

Are schools led by experts?

Goodall and Baker present a positive picture of the benefits which will be received by organisations led by experts in their field. By their definition, most schools are run by experts, in the sense that the vast majority of headteachers and senior leaders in schools are qualified teachers. Therefore, one might expect to find a utopia of working conditions for teachers across our education system, led by technical experts who understand the conditions required to optimise performance and wellbeing of core workers. And yet, not all of the theoretical benefits suggested by the authors of this paper are consistently present in our schools. Why should this be?

The contention of Section 1 of this book is that our education system is set up in such a way as to undermine the role of expertise in our schools. At a classroom level, we have pursued ideologies that downplay the importance of disciplinary knowledge. At a school level, we have shown an increasing lack of trust and respect for the 'expert-based intuition' of school leaders. At a system level, we have valued short-term, superficial measures of success over sustained value-building investment. To address this, expertise needs to be placed at the very heart of our efforts to improve schools. We will feel the full benefits of expert leadership if we:

- Recognise the fundamental importance of domain-specific knowledge for school leaders;
- Invest in developing genuine expertise in our leaders rather than abstract leadership competencies;
- Reduce the distractions faced by school leaders so that they can focus on making decisions which are in the best interests of their schools;
- Give leaders time and space to achieve meaningful improvement in their schools;
- Display confidence in school leaders, showing trust in their motives and expertise by removing unnecessarily heavy-handed accountability mechanisms.

Expert leadership cannot transform our education system overnight, but it is a necessary condition for sustained school improvement.

Summary of chapter substance

▬▬▬▬▬▬ Substance (stuff) What do we need to know?	Schools are highly complex organisations which require leadership expertise to be built on a deep knowledge of the domain. While intelligence, personality and attitude will enable leaders to survive in the short term, domain-specific knowledge must be acquired to be an effective leader. Leaders of teachers should themselves be teachers, as this will provide them with the credibility and insight needed to make good decisions and inspire others.
▬▬▬▬▬▬ Substance (significance) Why is this important?	A better understanding and greater respect for expertise, and an educational system which promotes it, is key to improving our schools.
▬▬▬▬▬▬ Substance (validity) How do we know it to be true?	There is considerable evidence from the field of cognitive science and expertise research to help understand how experts use their domain-knowledge to solve complex problems.

References

1. Geary, D. C. (2008) 'An Evolutionary Informed Education Science', *Educational Psychologist* 43 pp. 179-195.

2. Hawkins, M. and James, C. (2016) *Theorising schools as organisations: Isn't it all about complexity?* Paper presented at American Educational Research Association Annual Meeting, Washington, D.C. 8/04/16-12/04/16.

3. Schon, D. (1987) *Educating the Reflective Practitioner.* San Francisco, CA: Jossey-Bass.

4. Tricot, A. and Sweller, J. (2014) 'Domain-Specific Knowledge and Why Teaching Generic Skills Does Not Work', *Educational Psychology Review* p. 19.

5. Didau, D. (2019) *Making Kids Cleverer.* Carmarthen, Wales: Crown House Publishing,.

6. Tricot, A. and Sweller, J. (2014) 'Domain-Specific Knowledge and Why Teaching Generic Skills Does Not Work', *Educational Psychology Review* 26 (2) p. 265-283.

7. Ackerman, P. L. (2000) 'Domain-Specific Knowledge as the "Dark Matter" of Adult Intelligence: Gf/Gc, Personality and Interest Correlates', *Journal of Gerontology* 55B (2).

8. Goodall, H. and Baker, A. (2014) *A Theory Exploring How Expert Leaders Influence Performance in Knowledge-Intensive Organizations.* New York, NY: Springer, pp. 49-68.

9. Bradley, J. H., Paul, R. and Seeman, E. (2006) 'Analyzing the Structure of Expert Knowledge', *Info Manage* 43 (1) pp. 77-91.

10. Sembugamoorthy, V. and Chandresekaren, B. (1986) 'Functional Representation of Devices and Compilation of Diagnostic Problem-Solving Systems', in Kolodner, J. L. and Reisbeck, C. K. (eds) *Experience, Memory, and Reasoning.* Hillsdale, NJ: pp. 47-71.

11. Chase, W. G. and Simon, H. A. (1973) 'Perception in Chess', *Cognitive Psychology* 4 (1) pp. 55-81

12. de Groot, A. (1978) *Thought and Choice in Chess* (second edition). The Hague: Mouton De Gruyter.

13. Nonaka, I. and Takeuchi, H. (1995) *The Knowledge-Creating Company.* New York, NY: Oxford University Press.

14. Tichy, N. M. and Bennis, W. G. (2007) 'Making Judgement Calls', *Harvard Business Review* pp. 94-102.

15. Goodall, H. and Baker, A. (2014), *A Theory Exploring How Expert Leaders Influence Performance in Knowledge-Intensive Organizations.* New York City, NY: Springer, p. 3.

16. Artz, B., Goodall, A. H. and Oswald, A. J. (2014) 'Boss Competence and Worker Well-being', *IZA Discussion Papers*, No. 8559.

17. Artz, B., Goodall, A. H. and Oswald, A. J. (2016) If Your Boss Could Do Your Job, You're More Likely to Be Happy at Work, *Harvard Business Review* [Online], 29 December. Retrieved from: www.bit.ly/2intU2p

18. Robinson, V. M. J., Lloyd, C. A. and Rowe, K. J. (2008) 'The Impact of Leadership on Student Outcomes: An Analysis of the Differential Effects of Leadership Types', *Educational Administration Quarterly* 44 (5) pp. 635-674.

19. Mumford, M. D., Scott, G. M., Gaddis, B. and Strange, J. M. (2002) 'Leading Creative People: Orchestrating Expertise and Relationships', *Leadership Quarterly* 13 (6) pp. 705-750.

Chapter 10

What makes school leadership unique?

The most distinctive educational idea we have

Arguably, the most important concept that school leaders should seek to understand is that of the curriculum. The curriculum is what makes educational organisations distinct from all others, and therefore warrants particular attention. But not only is the curriculum unique to education, it also defines the very purpose of education as an endeavour. The curriculum is at the heart of schooling, and leaders who do not grasp this truth will be doomed to misdirect their efforts towards genericism.

The curriculum is an idea particular to education.[1] All organisations have a purpose, whether making people well (hospitals), dispensing justice (law courts), producing goods (factories), or protecting the vulnerable (social services), and there are mechanisms by which these organisations fulfil these purposes (e.g. medicinal treatment, court proceedings, production methods and social work). However, educational institutions fulfil their purpose with regard to the curriculum. Curriculum is the object of education; its transmission is the purpose, with pedagogy being the mechanism by which the purpose is delivered. Conceived of in this way, the curriculum adds a third dimension to educational institutions which is absent from other types of organisations: purpose, mechanism and <u>object</u>. The curricular object is fundamental to both the purpose and the mechanism; in other words, what we choose to teach is bound up with decisions about our school's goals and *how* we teach.

The curriculum is defined by what knowledge we want students to acquire, and this will depend on what we consider an 'educated person' to be. These decisions must not be taken lightly, or in isolation. Deciding the content of the curriculum is possibly the most important (or at least fundamental) decision schools must make. If school leaders are not fully part of, and equipped to understand, curriculum decisions, they will surrender their core leadership function and, thereby, their ability to define the school's purpose and meaningfully influence its practices. That is not to say that school leaders should control, or can even fully understand, every decision about how knowledge is selected, sequenced and imparted across the various subject disciplines; subject experts have a vital role to play in this process. However, school leaders must be sufficiently knowledgeable to engage meaningfully with subject experts such that decisions within each discipline are coherent with wider curriculum aims, and strategic curriculum decisions support the development of subject learning, rather than hinder it.

Powerful knowledge

How do we even begin to decide which knowledge should be selected for inclusion in the curriculum? At a strategic level, school leaders must decide which subjects to include in the curriculum and how much valuable curriculum time should be awarded to each. Within each subject, leaders must then decide what knowledge is most important for students to acquire. To some extent, these decisions are constrained by the availability of qualifications, exam board syllabuses, external examination requirements and, in some schools, the National Curriculum. However, schools have a high degree of autonomy over curriculum decisions, particularly pre-KS4, and school leaders must consider what knowledge is valued and is valuable.

The educationalist Michael Young[2] offers us the concept of 'powerful knowledge' as a way to avoid what he sees as misguided past attempts to define school curricula. Young criticises both the traditionalist approach to knowledge selection (which he terms Future 1) and the progressivist (Future 2) approach, which was discussed in Chapter 7. The Future 1 model sees the curriculum as a fixed extension of the past; a past in which the curriculum was a means by which privileged and able children progressed to elite universities. This approach was evident in the National Curriculum introduced in 1988 and, more recently, in Michael Gove's education policies. The Future 2 model emerged in response to the inflexibility of a traditionalist approach in an attempt to create an inclusive curriculum, accessible to those of all backgrounds and abilities. As participation in education beyond the age of 16 became compulsory, the challenges of engaging certain students in traditional subject disciplines led to a diversification of educational programmes which were designed to provide a 'pathway' for students to achieve their vocational ambitions. This instrumentalist view recast knowledge as being a means to an end, whether that end be a career destination or a place at a 'top' university. Arguably, rather than break down social inequality, the Future 2 model reinforced inequalities, as students from privileged backgrounds continued to pursue academic routes to higher education and those from disadvantaged backgrounds were channelled into low-status qualifications. Young sees Future 2 as the more objectionable of the two models, as the supposedly egalitarian attempt to place equal value on knowledge (whether it be the result of centuries of disciplined enquiry or the student's own personal experience) in reality reinforces social injustice and reduces social mobility.

Young offers a Future 3 as an alternative to the current swing back to a fixed, traditionalist view of the curriculum. Future 3 accepts that knowledge has social and historical routes and that it is not presented to us as given, as traditionalists would like us to believe. However, this does not mean that all knowledge is equal, or its value determined according to its worth to the individual; some knowledge is 'better' than other knowledge, in that it brings us closer to truth and understanding. In selecting literature for our school curriculum, we should not choose 'the classics' just because they are classified as such, but if they confer understanding of literature more successfully than the alternatives. In teaching the origins of our species, we should not merely teach Darwin's theory of evolution because it is part of the 'canon' of scientific theory, but because it has stood the test of time and proof to stand as scientific truth, or as close to the truth as we can get. The value of knowledge is not defined by its utility to the individual, nor by some authority which objectively weighs up the entirety of human knowledge and selects which propositions are worthiest of inclusion in our curriculum; rather valuation takes place through a continual process of review and refinement by the specialist communities whose purpose it is to create new knowledge and push the boundaries of human understanding. Specialist disciplinary knowledge, rather than being fixed, is continually re-evaluated, added to and re-conceptualised by those best placed to do so.

If schools exist to take students beyond their everyday experience and give them access to knowledge they would be unlikely to encounter in their day-to-day lives, then knowledge defined and valued by specialist disciplinary communities is, arguably, the most reliable source of content for our school curriculum. Furthermore, if social equality is a core purpose of our educational system, then ensuring that this curriculum is provided without favour to every child is a priority. This knowledge is powerful, because it takes us as close as the human species has been to truth and understanding. It is powerful for the individual, as it provides every young person with an equal opportunity to understand the world around them and, perhaps, to contribute to expanding the boundaries of human understanding themselves. Powerful knowledge is an intellectual resource. Young provides us with three criteria to help us recognise it:

- It is distinct from the 'common sense' knowledge we acquire through everyday experience;
- It is systematic, in that its concepts are related to each other in groups known as subjects or disciplines;
- It is specialised, i.e. developed by clearly distinguishable groups with a defined focus of enquiry.

This brief, theoretical excursion into educational philosophy risks over-intellectualising the pragmatic task of leading the school curriculum. However, Young is clear that he offers the concept of powerful knowledge as a practical tool for helping leaders make decisions about the curriculum:

I want to propose the concept of 'powerful knowledge' as a resource for heads in their curriculum leadership role, as a basis for an agreement in their school on 'what it should teach' as well as for achieving greater equality of outcomes and a more socially just society.

Without Young's ideas, we risk moving away from curricular genericism and falling back into the arms of a fixed, elitist view of curricular substance. Once we understand the importance and proper place of subject disciplines, we, as school leaders, need to know about the nature of these disciplines and their relation to the school curriculum.

Disciplines and subjects

If the school curriculum is to be drawn from bodies of knowledge defined by specialist disciplinary communities, school leaders need to understand the nature of these disciplines and how they relate to school subjects.

Disciplinary knowledge simply means the knowledge which is taught to pupils – the term 'discipline' originating from the Latin words *discipulus* (meaning pupil) and *disciplina* (meaning teaching).[3] However, disciplinary knowledge is formed in specialist communities often found in, or centred around, universities. This knowledge is grouped as 'academic disciplines', which is the term used to describe how knowledge is organised and new knowledge is developed within the field. The grouping of knowledge infers clear boundaries between each discipline, but in reality, academic disciplines are not easily delineated and are contested. However, academic disciplines tend to share common characteristics, including having an object of research, a distinct body of knowledge, including theories and concepts, specific terminology and specialist language, and particular research methods. There is an institutional aspect to defining academic disciplines too, as their existence is associated with formal, institutional structures which legitimise and ensure the continued existence of the discipline.

As opposed to an academic discipline, a 'subject discipline' refers to a taught body of knowledge usually associated directly with a specialist academic discipline. Subject disciplines (or 'subjects', as they are colloquially known in schools) derive and take their legitimacy from academic disciplines; however, they are not the same thing. Activity in academic disciplines is mostly in relation to the creation of new knowledge, whereas the focus of subject disciplines is the transmission of existing knowledge. The knowledge to be taught in subjects is selected from the disciplinary field following consideration of the learners' prior knowledge, ability to acquire new knowledge, and how the knowledge may be paced and sequenced coherently to achieve the desired educational goals. In addition to picking and choosing from the knowledge created by the academic disciplinary enquiry, subjects may also include the study of the method of enquiry itself to provide students with an understanding of the customs and practices of the academic discipline. However, it is important not to confuse the *study* of how new knowledge is created in the discipline with the *practice* of creating knowledge by attempting to make students 'rediscover' the established knowledge for themselves, or actually attempt to produce new knowledge. The purpose of subjects is to equip the next generation with the most powerful knowledge which exists in the discipline quickly and efficiently (through instruction) so that some may go on, as experts of the future, to push the boundaries of knowledge further (through enquiry). Before we can 'stand on the shoulders of giants', we must clamber up the giant.

The academic disciplines are distinct from each other in numerous ways and this, in turn, affects the nature of the subject discipline which draws on it. From a philosophical perspective, the differences relate to the nature of the knowledge within each discipline, how the knowledge is structured and organised, and how it relates to reality. Academic disciplines may be defined by whether they are 'hard' (e.g. scientific) or 'soft' (e.g. social), 'pure' (theoretical) or 'applied', or relating to living systems (e.g. biology) or non-living systems (e.g. history). Some fields are considered true disciplines as they strictly meet the criteria and have clear boundaries and academic histories, while others are considered weak disciplines, such as English literature, which lacks a 'unifying theoretical paradigm'. The importance and status of academic disciplines is also affected by their present utility (e.g. potential to make profit), longevity (such as the low status afforded to many academic disciplines established in the last century) or lack of theoretical content.

As Christine Counsell notes, curriculum leadership is 'fiendishly complex'.[4] This is, in no small part, due to the way in which subject disciplines relate to academic disciplines. She describes the way in which 'subjects are derived from the great traditions of knowledge construction in academic and artistic fields, each with its own rules of enquiry and evidence, its own traditions of argument and debate or its own standards of performance and judgement. Each echoes a distinctive quest for truth and each carries accumulated wisdom that must be mastered if its wider ways are to be opened up.' Navigating this complexity to determine the 'powerful knowledge' to form our curriculum requires significant disciplinary knowledge which even an expert subject leader will take years to acquire. What might we reasonably expect senior leaders to understand?

The challenge of senior curriculum leadership

We have, once again, arrived at the question of how senior leaders in schools can hope to lead in an educational system that leaves behind genericism and embraces subject disciplines and knowledge, which we last considered in Chapter 7. Whereas before, our focus was a critique of genericism and the barriers to leaving this orthodoxy behind, this chapter has made a positive case for an alternative, based on Young's conceptions of Future 3 and powerful knowledge[2]. I would like to build on the positive in the remainder of this chapter to suggest the practical ways school leaders may adjust their practice to meet the challenges laid down by the likes of Young and Counsell.

I previously argued that the shift from curricular genericism to 'curricular substance' (i.e. curriculum leadership concerned with subject disciplines and knowledge) will require us to radically rethink what senior curriculum leadership means, not least of all as it requires senior school leaders to accept that much of the curriculum knowledge required is (or will need to be) possessed by the curriculum expert (meaning the teacher and/or subject leader) and not the senior leader. This shift threatens/promises to transform the identity and practices of school leadership, particularly where leaders have created hierarchical structures which rely on top-down accountability mechanisms.

Although senior leaders are likely to feel threatened by such a fundamental re-conceptualisation of their role, and may actively resist this change, I would argue that we should perceive this as an opportunity. Placing knowledge at the centre of educational discourse and practice has the potential to enable leaders to focus on the meaningful rather than superficial abstract goals of recent years, such as league table positions, audit trails and data crunching. Leaders will be liberated from their managerial role and be better able to distribute decision-making throughout the organisation. This, in turn, should improve organisational culture by returning to the notion of a community of experts, and reduce leaders' workload as they shrug off omnipotence. Of course, some leaders have resisted genericism throughout this period but they have lived an uncomfortable existence, continually taking a stand against the prevailing orthodoxy, and many will have left the profession. But those who have held on to their beliefs and survived will feel vindicated if the tide changes in the way it appears to be.

Curriculum-focused leadership

The challenge of senior curriculum leadership is the challenge of achieving 'curriculum authenticity'. An authentic curriculum is not driven by the goal of achieving better examination results, or to make sure students 'get the grades they need' for the next stage of their education, or in order to stop students disengaging and opting out in the face of difficulty. Rather, it is a curriculum created from knowledge which is empowering, equitable and true, constructed with integrity and intellectual honesty.

The challenge of senior curriculum leadership is the challenge of creating a culture which values, cultivates and empowers subject specialists to recognise the essential truths and powerful knowledge in their subject domain, construct a curriculum narrative through which pupils will have meaningful encounters with this knowledge, and select instructional methods which enable all pupils to make sense of the curriculum to assimilate new knowledge into their mental schema.

Senior curriculum leadership in a Future 3 model[2] will require leaders to rethink many aspects of their practice.

Understanding subject domains

The first step for senior curriculum leaders aiming to respect disciplinary distinctiveness will be to equip themselves with sufficient knowledge of subjects and the academic disciplines from which they derive. This will be no small feat and we cannot expect senior leaders to develop the kind of expertise bestowed by a specialist degree-level qualification in each subject. However, it may be sufficient to seek to understand the differences between subjects in terms of their epistemic structures.

Senior leaders may begin by seeking answers to questions such as:

- What is the scope and nature of the knowledge accrued in the discipline?
- How does the discipline accrue this knowledge?
- How, and to what extent, is the substantive knowledge contested?
- What is the nature of evidence in the discipline?
- What concepts are fundamental to understanding the discipline (core knowledge)?
- How has knowledge from the discipline been selected for inclusion in the school curriculum?
- In what ways does knowledge build and interconnect to create a deep understanding?
- What considerations are there for sequencing how students encounter knowledge?
- In what ways does the nature of the subject affect its pedagogy?
- What controversies exist within the discipline and/or disciplinary community?
- How is the discipline affected by its history, political influences and social context?

The purpose of asking such questions is, firstly, to understand the curriculum so that better senior curriculum leadership can be achieved, and, secondly, to begin to understand whether others, such as the subject leader, have a solid grasp of the discipline and a detailed knowledge upon which they make curricular decisions.

Articulating priorities

Senior leaders will need to begin to articulate school aims in terms of substantive curriculum goals. Success, rather than being described in terms of examination outcomes or participation in higher education, may be expressed in terms of students acquiring powerful knowledge, having equal access to a curriculum entitlement, and those from disadvantaged backgrounds choosing to pursue high-status academic study beyond the school leaving age. Senior leaders will need to provide a compelling vision, underpinned by the pursuit of social justice, for a universal entitlement to a carefully constructed, well sequenced, subject-based curriculum.

The questions leaders ask

In holding others to account for delivering ambitious educational standards, the questions leaders ask will inevitably have to change. When visiting lessons, leaders will begin with the knowledge being taught rather than the teaching approaches employed, the apparent engagement of students, or evidence of their learning or progress. They may ask the teacher:

- Where does this knowledge fit into the narrative of the curriculum?
- What will students have to know before they can acquire this new knowledge and make sense of it? How do you know they are ready to do so?
- What cognitive challenge does this knowledge present and how will your teaching attempt to overcome this?
- How will this knowledge be reinforced and further developed?
- How will this knowledge be used in the future, and what will this learning enable students to understand better?

The quality of teaching cannot be judged separately from the content of the curriculum, as the pedagogy and knowledge are inextricably intertwined. Similarly, the leader will be interested as much in *what* the student is learning as *whether* they are learning. If we place the curriculum at the centre of schools, learning is no longer an end in itself. What has been learnt, its value and place in the curriculum, is critical to making judgements about the progress of students. Therefore, the nature of other common quality-assurance activities, such as work scrutiny, must also change. Rather than looking for evidence that students know or can do something which they previously did/could not, the nature of the knowledge acquired and how it builds over time will become the primary concern.

The data leaders collect

A respect for knowledge and disciplinary distinctiveness will also be reflected in the type of data leaders feel it necessary to collect. Data must convey meaning, and the challenge will be to find authentic ways to capture information about students' progress, where the conception of progress may differ between subjects, topics, or even items of knowledge. To separate 'progress data' from information about what has been learnt prevents any meaningful interpretation of the data by leaders. Fulfilling the leadership role of ensuring that students are making progress becomes far more complex when truth can no longer be inferred from numbers or grades.

Strategic curriculum choices

Senior leaders will need to rethink the curricular models which determine when students drop subjects and make choices to specialise. All students should study all subjects up until the point where the desired powerful knowledge has been taught and acquired. Once dropped, we should assume that the student may not encounter formal study of this discipline again, therefore we should be satisfied that they have acquired a sufficient foundation of knowledge of the field. The Future 3 model also raises questions about grouping, the content of the curriculum taught to each group and the pace at which the content is covered. While some students may take more time to move through the curriculum and acquire the desired knowledge, it is still their right to access the same content as others.

Leaders will also need to think carefully about the vocational courses on offer and be satisfied that these are not weak substitutes for academic programmes. For example, a leisure and tourism course might include concepts relating to economic development, the environmental damage caused by tourism and changes in income and demographics, which have led to shifts in how people spend their leisure time. Vocational programmes may be inter-disciplinary in relation to what knowledge is drawn upon, but the knowledge should still be powerful and fundamental to students' understanding of the world.

Professional development

Delivering curriculum authenticity will require time and resources to be spent on developing the disciplinary knowledge of teachers and allowing them time to make decisions about what knowledge to include in their subject curriculum and how this will be sequenced and taught. While there should still be time spent on pedagogy, the balance will shift towards curriculum development, and teachers' development of classroom practice will begin with an understanding of what is to be taught. As senior leaders are unlikely to hold all the expertise needed to provide the subject-specific professional development required, subject networks and associations will become increasingly important. The school leaders' role will be to facilitate teachers' access to subject and disciplinary communities and to encourage them to develop their own disciplinary knowledge.

Curriculum-focused leadership will likely look very different to current practice in schools and will require leaders to adapt their practices significantly. General theories of leadership will only be useful to an extent as a guide for school leaders during this period of change as they do not take account of the object of education: the curriculum. Without a clear conception of the curriculum, we cannot articulate a coherent vision for our schools, provide a compelling case for change or deliver school improvement. School leadership must be re-imagined to include the goal of curriculum authenticity if we are to provide access to powerful knowledge for all our young people.

Summary of chapter substance

▬▬▬▬▬▬ **Substance (stuff)** What do we need to know?	School leadership is unique, in that only educational organisations have a curriculum, and this curriculum is fundamental to the school's purpose and operations. Disciplinary knowledge should be the basis of the school curriculum, and understanding the power of knowledge is essential for school leaders in developing the curriculum and delivering social justice. However, making 'curriculum authenticity' a central goal of schools will require leaders to radically re-imagine their role in delivering school improvement.
▬▬▬▬▬▬▬ **Substance (significance)** Why is this important?	The curriculum is, arguably, the most important consideration for school leaders. If we lead the curriculum well, education will be transformational for young people; particularly the socially disadvantaged.
▬▬▬▬▬▬ **Substance (validity)** How do we know it to be true?	The traditionalist and progressive ideologies which have driven conceptions of the curriculum in recent decades have failed to deliver real improvement or tackle social inequality. And yet we have access to 'the best' of human knowledge, tried and tested by specialist disciplinary communities, which can be utilised by schools as the basis for an enriching and empowering curriculum.

References

1. Young, M. and Lambert, D. (2014) *Knowledge and the Future School*. London: Bloomsbury.

2. Ibid.

3. Krishnan, A. (2009) *What are Academic Disciplines?* Southampton: National Centre for Research Methods.

4. Counsell, C. (2018) 'In search of senior curriculum leadership: Introduction – a dangerous absence', *The dignity of the thing* [Online], 27 March. Retrieved from: www.bit.ly/30UsTRH

Chapter 11

Portraying purpose

'The function of education... is to teach one
to think intensively and to think critically. But
education which stops with efficiency may
prove the greatest menace to society. The
most dangerous criminal may be the man
gifted with reason, but with no morals.'
- Dr. Martin Luther King Jr., *The Purpose of Education* (1947)[1]

What is the point of school? Many people have tried to answer this question, but doing so is not my concern. My interest lies in how school leaders portray the purpose of education to engage the efforts of their followers.

'Influence' is cited frequently in the literature on leadership as the primary way in which leaders ensure that followers direct their efforts towards the desired goals. In most models of leadership, influence is seen as preferable to the use of power to control (often termed 'authoritarianism'). We can agree that creating an environment in which people want to achieve shared goals is more desirable in our schools than the use of coercive behaviours. The very notion of leadership implies the concept of followership, and we rightly imagine these followers coming willingly, rather than being bound and chained.

Effective leaders form a kind of social contract with their followers. The contract asks for followers to trust in the leader and subscribe to their vision for the school. In return, the leader promises to deliver a better future – one in which the follower can see benefits in working towards. Thinking of this relationship as a contract can be seen as reducing it to a transactional basis where each side pursues a personal gain, but we need not exclude altruistic desires from this model. Both teachers and school leaders will have a moral motivation for the job they do, and the social contract will likely be formed from a shared goal to create better opportunities for the children at the school. Social contracts are the means by which leaders influence, and their leadership is only effective as long as, and to the extent that, these social contracts hold.

Influence is a neutral act[2] in that it can be used for good or ill. We cannot, therefore, claim that influence is a desirable trait for leaders in and of itself. The ability to influence must be considered alongside the purposes the leader pursues and the way their influence is employed; both of which depend on the values held by the leader. Values transform influence from a neutral into a moral quality. But what is interesting about the relationship between values and influence is not just that values give influence meaning and worth, but that the leader's values will determine, to some extent, whether influence is attained and retained. For followers to succumb to the influence of the leader, for the social contract to be formed, they will need to subscribe to the values espoused by the leader, to at least some degree. The leader's values are, therefore, inextricably bound to their ability to influence; they must find common moral ground with their followers to earn legitimacy and credibility. While we are appointed to a position of authority, influence is in the gift of those we lead.

Our understanding of influence as a leadership trait suggests that the way a leader sees and portrays the purpose of education, in particular the purpose of the school being led, is critical to their success in influencing others and bringing about desirable change. It is no surprise, therefore, that the idea of 'vision' has become a stalwart of leadership literature and training.

Compelling visions

Dr. Martin Luther King Jnr., quoted above, was perhaps the master of rhetoric when it came to portraying a vision. In 1963, King professed his 'dream' to the multitudes assembled in Washington D.C.; a vision of a future in which 'my four little children will one day live in a nation where they will not be judged by the color of their skin but by the content of their character'.[3] What made King's vision so compelling was his ability to describe a better version of the world, rooting this in a belief held true by the American people and embedded in their very constitution: that 'all men are created equal'. King spoke with conviction and urgency, contrasting his bold imaginings with the harsh realities of discrimination and prejudice for racial minorities in the U.S.

Few can deny that compelling visions, such as that portrayed by King, play an important role in social reform. However, what role should they play in schools?

The empirical evidence regarding the importance of vision in leadership is mixed,[4] and there are risks involved for leaders in articulating a strong vision, as others may not share the dream, or the assumptions on which it is based. To consider why vision might do more harm than good, I will explore three problems:

1. Visions without substance.

2. Visions of heroes.

3. Visions not lived.

Visions without substance

Consider the following statements, each taken from the published vision of real schools:

'Two years to Outstanding'

'Good is the enemy of Excellence'

'We will ensure our capacity to rapidly improve the quality of teaching and learning through harnessing the learning power of four key competencies: Resilience, Resourcefulness, Reflectiveness and Reciprocity across the curriculum.'

Consider which, if any, of these schools you would like to work in. Each reflects aspects of leadership genericism described in Section 1. The first example is notable by the use of the capital 'O' in Outstanding, inferring the aim of securing a particular Ofsted grade rather than attaining exceptional educational standards. A generous interpretation of this goal is that the school's leaders believe that these two aims are one and the same: that Ofsted's judgements are so reliable and valid that their accreditation of the school's work will prove the existence of superior standards in every aspect of provision. That may be, but why select this badge of honour as the goal rather than the actual achievement of standards which stand out from the crowd? The isomorphic pressures to look good over being good can lead to a superficial vision of what the school aspires to become. This may signal ambition to the community, but is it a compelling moral purpose which will inspire those in the school to go the extra mile?

But the second example would suggest that neither looking or being good is enough: good is the 'enemy'. This vision calls for all members of the school's community to adopt a heroic and uncompromising standard against which to measure themselves (or be measured). While admirably ambitious, what psychological pressure would the enactment of this vision have in practice? We might imagine the teacher saying, 'That is a good piece of homework, Johnny, but good is our enemy... next time I need excellence!' Or the feedback from a teacher's recent lesson observation where they have failed, again, to be rated 'excellent' in every category. Such visions become a dystopian nightmare for those compelled to follow them.

By comparison, the third example appears fairly harmless. However, what substance is there to this vision? Do the objects of improvement, expressed conveniently as all words beginning with 'R', really capture the purpose of the school, and what evidence is there to support the 'learning power' of these competencies? The teachers in such a school, targeted with delivering these alliterative goals, are identified as the engine for achieving the school's vision as they 'rapidly improve' teaching and learning. But if this improvement doesn't take place, it won't be the fault of the school's leaders, as they will have 'ensured the capacity' for improvement, rather than actually improving anything.

Before you accuse me of purposefully searching out the worst examples of school vision statements, let me point out that all the above were cited as examples (presumably of good practice) by the National College for Teaching and Leadership[5] as part of their suite of resources for leadership development. Among the examples given were some far more palatable statements of intent, for example:

In our college, we value and respect every person as a child of God, as we grow together in faith, knowledge, understanding and love to serve the community.

Whether or not you hold religious beliefs, here is a school we might like to work for.

In portraying a vision, school leaders must take great care that it has substance and integrity. Given that one of the main purposes of a vision is as the basis for the social contract between the leader and their followers, the strength of which determines their influence as a leader, the inferred goals must be worthwhile, meaningful and achievable.

Visions of heroes

A further problem for leaders is to be able to articulate a vision which genuinely reflects the hopes and dreams of all those in the school community. Although school leaders might be on a moral crusade, they should remember that they are not the only one with morals, or with fire in their belly. We came across this problem when considering the concept of 'transformational leadership' and the rise of the 'hero head'. In order to form a vision which is truly shared, school leaders must have an understanding of the values and aspirations of the community they serve. The role of the leader is not to dream up a vision, but to act like a magnifying glass, channelling the sunlight to create focused energy. Seeing oneself as the conduit for the collective view of what the school could become, rather than as the source of the vision, helps ensure humility in leadership and reminds us that our influence is borrowed.

Visions not lived

The current fashion for publishing our carefully worded vision, placing it on the school website, banners and all over the prospectus, undoubtedly, is the result of the pressures on schools to market themselves. As a parent, we may welcome this, as it provides information about what the school stands for and helps us decide whether it is a good fit with our values and ambitions for our children. These pronouncements can become an albatross around the neck of leaders, quoted back at them by disgruntled parents or staff. This is inevitable, to some extent, but school leaders must work hard to ensure that their actions are consistent with the published vision. To achieve this coherence, even among the senior leadership team, is difficult enough, but leaders must constantly reinforce, with all staff, the importance of behaving in certain ways. Values can serve as a means by which to portray these expectations, and the school vision should make clear, or be presented alongside, a clear explanation of the core values of the school.

Where staff experience inconsistency between the school's stated values and the actions of leaders, the social contract will deteriorate and leaders will gradually lose their influence, increasingly having to rely on authority and formal power to ensure that staff act in the way expected. Articulating a meaningful and worthwhile purpose, underpinned by strong values which leaders model in their everyday actions, is essential in creating a positive, professional culture. Where this is missing, schools can quickly slide into managerial and autocratic leadership styles.

We should be cautious about vision; it is too easy to get it wrong. I prefer to think in terms of 'purpose'. Purpose does not have to be all encompassing (like a grand vision), but everything we do will have purpose, and we should take the time to remind ourselves what it is. By asking the question 'what are we trying to achieve?' in any given situation, we can usually agree and unite around a common purpose. This question prompts us to constantly renew the social contract, reminding us that we are on the same team and have, broadly if not exactly, the same goals. Considering our purpose also forces us to revisit the values on which we base our actions. When observing a colleague teach, we should remember that both observer and teacher have the same purpose: to develop practice. We don't need a vision to remind us that effective teaching is important. When discussing the right sanction for a child who has been rude to a teacher, we should remind ourselves that the purpose is to teach children how to behave respectfully towards others. This sentiment comes from a position of human decency and common sense, not because our mission statement says we will instil respect. Portraying a moral purpose in everything we do will beat vision statements hands-down in creating strong social contracts and influencing others to go above and beyond to achieve school improvement.

Moral leadership

Morality is one of the antidotes to leadership genericism in schools. Moral leadership is where authority and influence are derived from defensible conceptions of what is right or good.[6] Sergiovanni's description captures the approach advocated so far in this chapter:

> The school must move beyond concern for goals and roles to the task of building purposes into its structure and embodying these purposes in everything that it does with the effect of transforming school members from neutral participants to committed followers. The embodiment of purpose and the development of followership are inescapably moral.[7]

Moral leadership is closely related to the idea of transformational leadership, although less centred around a single leader and more aligned with democratic values. School leadership is a necessarily moral enterprise as it is concerned with human development and fulfilment, and school leaders are therefore required to be 'morally confident', meaning having the capacity to act in a way that is consistent with an ethical system and over time. School leaders must:

- demonstrate causal consistency between principle and practice
- apply principles to new situations
- create shared understanding and a common vocabulary
- explain and justify decisions in moral terms
- sustain principles over time
- reinterpret and restate principles as necessary.[8]

However, despite affiliating myself to this leadership perspective, I believe we need to be cautious in demanding a renewed morality among school leaders when the education system makes it very difficult for leaders to do what is right.

In 2019, the grandly titled ASCL Ethical Leadership Commission published their final report, which set out a moral framework for school leadership 'to support leaders in their decision-making and in calling out unethical behaviour'.[9] This is a laudable piece of work and I have some sympathy, as explained above, for their call for more ethical leadership practices in our education system. However, it strikes me that the attempt to improve ethical behaviour might be better achieved in other ways. The stated intention is to promote more ethical behaviour by inviting leaders to sign up to the framework, embedding it in development programmes and creating forums for ethical debate; the intention being that 'the language of values and virtues (become) part of everyday decision-making'. These actions suggest that the cause of unethical behaviour is that leaders aren't aware of these values and virtues, don't possess them in sufficient amounts and/or fail to consider ethical dimensions when making decisions.

I know of leaders who display the above deficiencies on a regular basis, but they are few and far between. Most school leaders I have known are acutely aware of the ethical dilemmas they face and have a strong moral compass.

Decision-making in education becomes corrupted not as a result of the moral deficiencies of school leaders, but systemic pressures which divert leaders from acting solely in the best interests of students. Immoral behaviour is a rational response to perverse incentives. Such perverse incentives abound in the education system. It is structural deficiencies, mostly in relation to accountability measures, which have resulted in 'gaming' results, off-rolling, fraud and a range of other immoral practices. We should approach these problems as economists, not moral philosophers, if we want substantial change to occur.

None of this is to say that a clear, ethical framework isn't desirable, or that school leaders should not be held to these high standards. We need strong moral leadership in education more than ever, and headteachers need to do what is right. This can mean an irrational disregard for how the school is judged and even for one's own job security and wellbeing. But if we really want to make education a more moral endeavour, let's start by addressing the system within which human agents make decisions. The easier we make it for leaders to act ethically, the more they will do so.

The object of leadership influence

Let's imagine that we have secured the confidence and trust of others; influence is ours. What should we do with this influence? What is its subject? These are moral questions, but they are also questions about substance, in that leadership needs an object.

Central to the decision about how influence should be used is the question of whether leaders should exercise their influence directly or indirectly. Direct influence is exercised by leaders intervening with the core business of teachers, which is usually assumed to be teaching and learning. Indirect influence involves a concern with the broader school climate: creating the conditions in which teachers can perform their role.

Both direct and indirect influence by leaders has been termed 'instructional leadership'[10] in school management literature; the emphasis on one over the other varying according to how it is defined. A 'narrow' view emphasises the benefits of school leaders directly influencing teaching practice, while a 'broad' view is often seen as more likely to allow a range of professionals to exert influence, and therefore is in keeping with the social culture traditionally found in schools. Direct influence over the core business of teachers is an attractive idea, particularly where there is pressure to improve standards in a school quickly, but its impact may be limited by two factors in particular:

1. The locus of expertise

The question of where expertise lies, as discussed in Chapter 9, is relevant to this issue. While we may argue for the benefits of 'expert leadership', meaning it is desirable for school leaders to be technically competent in the core business of the school, this does not mean that they know better than the individual teachers about classroom practice; neither is this the reason cited for needing expert knowledge. The core argument for expert leadership is that leaders will understand what conditions are needed in order for experts to flourish – it is an argument for a broader conception of direct influence, one where the leader influences the wider working environment. To add weight to this argument, we must also recognise the issue of disciplinary distinctiveness, as outlined in Chapter 10. While it is desirable for school leaders to know enough about the differences between subject disciplines to fulfil their function as senior curriculum leaders, they cannot possibly hope to know as much as the subject experts in every field. Schools which have lost sight of the locus of expertise operate on the false belief that school leaders know more than classroom teachers about teaching and learning; they have come to believe in generic concepts of pedagogy, separate from the discipline and classroom context. This is a comforting belief, as it legitimises intervention and control, which satisfies the requirement to act quickly and assertively – to be seen to be 'doing something' about standards. However, this misunderstanding will gradually undermine the social contract between teacher and leader, and ultimately usurp the leader's influence.

2. The object of influence

Instructional leadership often assumes the object to be teaching and learning. The focus on generic teaching and learning practices in schools, played out through accountability systems and professional development, is, arguably, the wrong object of leadership efforts. In Chapter 10, we considered an alternative perspective: that the proper object of leadership should be the knowledge being taught, not just the means of its transmission. The way teachers instruct students, organise their classrooms and create a climate for learning is, of course, important, but failing to acknowledge that teachers' practices are fundamentally driven by what is being taught means that leadership efforts to directly influence what teachers do will be misguided, even damaging, to learning.

When we avoid the distraction of genericism and instead look for substance, we find that we may be influencing the wrong things in the wrong way. The moral and informed leader will recognise the limits of their expertise and focus their efforts on indirectly influencing the working environment for teachers, such that expertise is allowed to flourish. Influence is gifted to leaders and its misuse will not be tolerated for long.

A preoccupation with 'teacher effectiveness' and a tendency to scrutinise it endlessly is a sign that school leadership has been corrupted in some way. We have increasingly relied on authority over influence, grand visions over moral purpose, targets over values, leadership over expertise and heroism over humility. We should find modest purpose in all that we do and look after our influence as we would a precious item borrowed from a friend.

Summary of chapter substance

▬▬▬▬▬▬ **Substance (stuff)** What do we need to know?	School leaders must portray a moral purpose in everything they do. This purpose must be meaningful and worthwhile; one which followers can subscribe and commit to. The education system should be set up to respect the expertise of leaders and teachers if we are to expect our schools to maintain ethical standards.
▬▬▬▬▬▬ **Substance (significance)** Why is this important?	Schools can be tempted to pursue superficial and morally indefensible aims at the expense of the school culture and long-term benefits for children.
▬▬▬▬▬▬ **Substance (validity)** How do we know it to be true?	The literature on school vision and multiple examples of school vision statements pay testament to a corrupt and shallow vision for our education system.

References

1. A transcript of King's Morehouse College student paper can be found here: www.bit.ly/30RnavS

2. Bush, T. and Glover, D. (2014) 'School leadership models: What do we know?', *School Leadership & Management* 34 (5) pp. 1-19

3. A transcript of Martin Luther King Jr's famous speech can be found here: www.bit.ly/2fmjJXA

4. Ibid (n 2)

5. National College for Teaching and Leadership. (No date) 'Developing the Vision', National College for School Leadership [Online]. Retrieved from: www.bit.ly/2AROQq6

6. Bush, T. and Glover, D. (2003) School Leadership: Concepts and Evidence. Nottingham: National College for Teaching and Leadership.

7. Sergiovanni, T. (1984) 'Leadership and Excellence in Schooling', *Educational Leadership* 41 (5) pp. 4-13.

8. West-Burham, J. (1997) 'Leadership for Learning: Re-engineering "Mind Sets"', *School Leadership and Management* 17 (2) pp. 231-243.

9. The Ethical Leadership Commission (2019) *Navigating the Educational Moral Maze.* London: The Chartered College of Teaching.

10. Sheppard, B. (1996) 'Exploring the Transformational Nature of Instructional Leadership', *Alberta Journal of Educational Research* 42 (4) pp. 325-44.

Chapter 12
Empathy

You listen as they begin to tell you what it has been like these past months: the crippling anxiety, panic attacks and mornings when their body just wouldn't get them out of bed. They get a little tearful at times, and you reach for the box of tissues that you always keep to hand for such moments. Your body language is open and you say very little – better to just let them talk, to get it all out. It will have been hard enough for them to have summoned up the courage to walk through the door. When they are spent, you allow what they have told you to settle. You ask a gentle question, chosen carefully to signal that you have been listening and want to understand. The monologue becomes a discussion. They appear to relax a little, share a joke, apologise for being so emotional... 'you've got enough on your plate,' they tell you. When you reach a natural end, you agree to talk again next week.

As they leave, one of your serial moaners is pacing anxiously outside your door. 'Can I speak to you for a minute please?'; it is a rhetorical question. Ten minutes later, depleted and frustrated at the pettiness of their concerns, you manage to manoeuvre them from your office. Thank goodness you kept your cool. They left, thinking you give a damn; every ounce of your emotional control went into that one. You flick open your emails just as a message from a parent pings into your inbox. 'Why does your school not care about my daughter?' – the subtext rather than a literal reading. You click 'reply' and begin to type... 'Dear Mrs Payne, thank you for bringing your concerns to my attention...'

When we engage with the world, what determines our response? What meaning do we make of the information coming in?

Our natural response to the first encounter described would be concern. What they are telling us sounds pretty dreadful; we want to alleviate their distress in some way. We will likely feel an emotional response, possibly even shedding a tear, too. Perhaps we have experienced some of the symptoms they are describing. This will increase our empathic reaction, taking us back to our own experiences; we know a little of what it might feel like for them. Or perhaps we have never experienced such things ourselves, but we have some idea of how they might feel, as we have known others who have gone through similar things. We have seen, first-hand, how anxiety and depression can impact on people's lives, and know a little about how they have overcome this.

As we engage with the next colleague, and then the parent, our emotional reaction is different. Affected by the first encounter, the concerns raised seem trivial. Our emotional capacity is wearing thin, but our rational mind takes over and we know that it will not be constructive to show impatience. How useful has our faculty for empathy been to us?

Making sense

Our minds assimilate new information by attaching it to what we already know. The process of assimilation is what gives meaning to the incoming information; in other words, we 'make sense' of new information by searching our mental schema and figuring out where it fits. To which part of our vast expanse of knowledge does this belong? For this reason, we will all interpret new information in different ways, attaching different meaning to what we see or hear. For those with personal experience of mental illness, hearing of someone else's difficulties will likely connect with our memory of our own experience, provoking an 'emotional' response. Even without such personal experiences, we are more likely to make sense of the person's predicament if we have a pre-existing understanding of such matters. Either way, the process of making meaning is determined by the prior knowledge held in mind.

Many reading this may find it to be an unappealing, reductionist view of our response to other human beings, but understanding what happens in the mind when we interact with the outside world is important in avoiding misconceptions about how we relate to others, and to our environment.

The myth of emotional intelligence

The idea of emotional intelligence (EI) has gained a popular following. EI is frequently cited as an important ability for leaders to possess. The concept is often associated with high levels of empathy and emotional control, therefore enabling those who have it to relate well to others and maintain a positive, controlled response in stressful situations; they can 'keep their head while all those around are losing theirs and blaming it on you' – we'll call this the Kipling Quality (from the poem *If*).

The problem is that there is no reliable evidence to suggest that emotional intelligence exists, let alone that it is a vital quality for leaders.

One of the most vocal critics of EI as a field of research is John Antonakis at the University of Lausanne. We have come across Antonakis before (in Chapter 3) in relation to his work on intelligence. Antonakis critiques the research around EI robustly and finds no reliable evidence that the concept offers anything distinct from a general notion of intelligence ('g'), and, furthermore, concludes that claims that EI is a necessary leadership quality are 'unsubstantiated, exaggerated, misrepresented, or simply false'.[1]

To understand Antonakis' perspective, it is important to note that he is not suggesting that leaders should ignore the emotional states of others, but that the emotional appraisal and social skills needed by leaders will be possessed by most normal human beings. In other words, these qualities are biologically primary, in that there is no special or hard-to-acquire knowledge or skill needed to be able to relate emotionally to other people. He argues that there is no need to have exceptional 'abilities' in this area; indeed, that there is evidence to suggest that to be overly empathic might negatively affect the performance of those being led.[2] Rather than high levels of EI, Antonakis suggests that leaders will create affective links with their followers through conveying a vision, moral conviction, a disposition towards holding high responsibilities, courage and confidence (corresponding to the arguments made in the last chapter).

The natural ability shown to relate emotionally to others involves the leader in interpreting and making judgements about the emotional state of the other person; this is known as 'social gauging ability'. Psychologists working in this field employ the concept of 'scripts' to explain how we do this. A script is an expectation about how events will occur and be ordered, which exist as part of our mental schema. Scripts are generalised knowledge constructed through repeated exposure to numerous similar events over a period of time[3] (similar to how we described procedural fluency arising from domain-specific practice in Chapter 2). The ability to learn scripts is believed to be related to our general intelligence, but the availability of these will also be determined by the level of exposure; in other words, the ability to relate to others in an emotional situation will depend on knowledge acquired through repeated experiences which are similar in nature to the present scenario.[4] Social gauging and emotional responsiveness are gained through life experience and do not require 'high EI' or particular empathic abilities. It would appear that what we label 'emotional intelligence' is simply general intelligence directed at emotional phenomena.[5]

What of the Kipling Quality – emotional control? There is no reason to believe that high levels of emotional control are anything more than socially learnt behaviours, like empathy. Antonakis makes a qualified argument for the downside of emotional control, arguing that it is sometimes beneficial for the leader to express negative emotions such as sadness, frustration and anger, as a basis for emotional appeals. However, such displays of emotion should be used sparingly by leaders, lest they create undue angst and negativity among followers. We learn when to keep our cool and when to let our true emotions leak, but there is no reason to think that this is some form of intelligence.

Against empathy

Our capacity to relate emotionally to people appears to be a natural human tendency to gauge the emotional state of others, then draw on our understanding and mental scripts to guide us in our response. This explanation, although a little unromantic, appears to rationally explain empathy. However, we tend to experience empathy in different ways. Some of us appear to grasp the distress of others but remain relatively unmoved ourselves, while some seem to actually share the emotions of the person they are empathising with. Which of these is a true empathetic response, and which is preferable? How sensitive and sympathetic should leaders be towards their followers?

Empathy is almost always portrayed through the media, arts, social sciences and in popular culture as a 'good thing'. However, in a book provocatively titled *Against Empathy: The Case for Rational Compassion*, Paul Bloom[6] sets out the arguments against a particular form of empathy. Bloom provides two alternative definitions of empathy:

Emotional empathy: the act of coming to experience the world as you think someone else does.

Cognitive empathy: an understanding that you are in pain without feeling it yourself.

Bloom presents a compelling argument against emotional empathy as being beneficial beyond a narrow set of circumstances. He presents emotional empathy as introducing bias into our thinking: focusing on individuals rather than the many, the anecdote over the aggregate, the near in preference to the far away, and the here and now instead of the long term. For example, when we hear of a plane crash killing hundreds of European citizens, we feel the horror of their fate and the suffering of their families. However, we give little thought to the thousands killed each year in road traffic accidents across the world. There is something about the single, shocking incident and our ability to imagine ourselves in the position of those passengers which arouses our sympathies. By contrast, accumulated, frequent events, often happening to people a long way away, who live very different lives to us, fails to provoke our compassion in quite the same way.

Moral philosophers have pointed to empathy as the source of righteous action; that somehow experiencing the emotions of others provokes us into an ethical response. Bloom paints a striking picture of coming across a boy struggling in a lake. Naturally, we wade in to help the boy. But are our actions motivated by our imagining ourselves in his position, our mouth filling up with water as we struggle to stay afloat, or by picturing the grief of his parents as they hear the news of his demise? Of course not. We act out of a sense of morality and compassion; a knowledge that to walk on by would be wrong and unthinkable. Bloom reminds us that there are many motivations for doing good in the world, and kindness arises from moral thought, intelligence, the capacity for self-control and a rational compassion for our fellow human beings. He describes our ability for rational compassion thus:

There is the capacity to understand what's going on in others people's heads, to know what makes them tick, what gives them joy and pain, what they see as humiliating or ennobling.

Bloom describes an empathy which requires some emotional detachment, but which in no way denies morality, compassion, kindness and love; indeed, he argues that such cognitive empathy will be to the greater benefit of humankind.

If we want our leaders to connect to their followers and act in their interests, rather than reach for the box of tissues and join them in wiping away tears, we should promote a more detached, cognitive empathy; one in which leaders are able to take the long view, less inclined to the knee-jerk response and prioritising the few over the many.

The veil of ignorance

We need our school leaders to show rational compassion. That is not to say that they should hide their humanity or turn off their emotional responses, but rather recognise that a more measured approach should be taken when making decisions. In the here and now, leaders may use simple delaying tactics to give them the space they need to make a balanced assessment of the dilemma. For larger decisions, such as policy making, leaders will need to develop ways of weighing up competing interests and priorities, including the impact the policy may have on different parties.

A useful thought experiment for the purpose of rationally empathic policy making was proposed by the American philosopher John Rawls[7] and is known as the Veil of Ignorance. In the experiment, those making policy decisions imagine waking up the next day in the position of any of the people who may be affected by the policy. By placing themselves 'in the shoes' of each individual or group, and being ignorant of the place in the society, community or hierarchy in which they will find themselves, the decision-maker will be moved towards a socially just policy which balances the interests of all parties. A simpler version of this problem is one I have termed the Coca-Cola problem. It arises from the dilemma I faced many times as a parent of two children in sharing a can of Coke equally between them (as this was a rare privilege, and I would only ever stretch to buying one can). After I had tried many times to pour this precious nectar equally between glasses, always leaving one child complaining that they had received less than their sister, I finally employed the Veil of Ignorance. One child would pour and the other would choose. This provided the ultimate incentive for the pourer to divide the drink equally, as they were not sure which glass they would end up with. Suddenly, both children felt that justice had been done.

Applying this thought experiment in practice is tricky, and let's not pretend we possess the ability to imagine ourselves into the heads of every member of our school community. However, it takes us closer to making policies which have social justice at their core, rather than just considering decisions from the perspective of ourselves, or those who are likely to benefit. In a school context, the Veil of Ignorance might be applied to decisions around setting students by ability (weighing the cost and benefits to high, medium and low attainers), exclusions (balancing the needs of the victim, perpetrator and wider community), or reward systems (considering the impact on those who do not receive rewards rather than just those who do).

The informed leader

Empathy, in the desirable sense that we are able to show compassion and kindness without bias, and to the benefit of all those we lead, requires leaders to possess knowledge: knowledge of emotional states; knowledge of the personal histories and circumstances of those they lead; knowledge of the difficulties members of school communities will often encounter; knowledge of how such difficulties may be overcome and knowledge of the jobs that people do and the important role they play in the success of the school. Without knowledge, there is no understanding, and without this, no rational basis for compassion can exist.

If the leaders we open up to lack the knowledge to understand what we are telling them, we will not feel heard. We all possess the ability to 'listen' in the sense of sitting still and directing our attention to the words someone says, but the real skill is in making sense of what we are being told. Listening is a leadership competency that requires knowledge.

If leaders make decisions with apparent disregard to the consequences for individuals or groups, we will not trust them. Anyone can make a decision, but good decisions take account of the impact they will have on those subject to them. Trust is created and maintained by leaders who make compassionate and informed decisions.

Empathy masquerades as a soft skill, but it has a solid core. We should reach for understanding before we reach for the tissues.

Summary of chapter substance

▬▬▬▬▬▬ **Substance (stuff)** What do we need to know?	There is no special talent called Emotional Intelligence that leaders must possess. We all have the ability to empathise, and leaders should develop their emotional capacity by seeking to understand others, not by sharing their pain. Leaders should exercise a rational compassion for all those in the school, and make just decisions based on a deep knowledge of the school's community.
▬▬▬▬▬▬ **Substance (significance)** Why is this important?	An overly emotional empathic response introduces bias in decision-making and clouds judgement.
▬▬▬▬▬ **Substance (validity)** How do we know it to be true?	The evidence to support processes such as social gauging and the use of mental scripts is much stronger than the evidence to support notions of emotional intelligence.

References

1. Antonakis, J. (2004) 'On Why "Emotional Intelligence" Will Not Predict Leadership Effectiveness Beyond IQ or the "Big 5": An Extension and Rejoinder', *Organizational Analysis* 12 (2) pp. 171-182.

2. Feyerhern, A. E. and Rice, C. L. (2002) 'Emotional Intelligence and Team Performance: The Good, the Bad and the Ugly', *The International Journal of Organizational Analysis* 10 (4) pp. 343-362.

3. Antonakis, J. (2003) 'Why "Emotional Intelligence" Does Not Predict Leadership Effectiveness: A Comment on Prati, Douglas, Ferris, Ammeter, and Buckley', *The International Journal of Organizational Analysis* 11 (4) pp. 355-361.

4. Abelson, R. P. (1981) 'Psychological Status of the Script Concept', *American Psychologist* 36 (7) pp. 715-729.

5. Becker, T. (2003) 'Is Emotional Intelligence a Viable Concept?', *Academy of Management Review* 28 (2) pp. 192-195.

6. Bloom, P. (2016) *Against Empathy: The Case for Rational Compassion.* London: Penguin Random House.

7. Rawls, J. (1971) *A Theory of Social Justice.* Cambridge, MA: Harvard University Press.

Chapter 13

Scripts

Imagine a typical day in the life of your school. Now imagine that the day is a play for which you are the director. The opening scene sees the students arriving; perhaps emptying from buses or greeting friends as they walk through the gate. The staff are also arriving, mostly by car and carrying bags of marking from the night before. As the omniscient director, you see all of this unfolding – little change from the day before. You notice two cars arriving at the same time and parking next to each other. One is your deputy head and the other a recently appointed NQT. They climb out of their cars and make brief eye contact but do not exchange a greeting. Your deputy quickly heads towards the building while the NQT goes to the boot of her car and removes what appears to be a heavy, plastic box full of resources. As she struggles to hold the box and shut the boot, a student approaches and offers to carry it for the teacher. The teacher smiles and accepts the offer; they walk away from the car together in conversation.

As director, how happy are you with the scene you watched play out? You are taken with the student coming to the aid of the new teacher; this is the kind of thing you'd like to see more of your students doing. But the exchange between the teacher and your deputy is a concern. So you run the scene again, this time with a few changes to the script. You give some direction to your deputy, telling her to give more warmth to her character. The cars arrive again, right on cue, and pull up into parallel spaces. They both exit their cars and, as before, make brief eye contact. The NQT looks away, unsure how to react. 'Morning,' your deputy says. Your new teacher returns the greeting as she heads to the boot of her car. 'How have you settled in so far?' says your deputy, before noticing the teacher struggling with what appears to be a very heavy box. 'Here, let me give you a hand with that.'

If only it were as easy as changing the script and giving some direction on character development.

We came across the term 'script' in the last chapter, used to describe the mental model someone follows when gauging and responding to the emotional state of another. Of course, there isn't a literal script in the sense of dialogue in a play; there is a 'heuristic', which our mind follows, like a trail bike following in the well-worn tracks in a dirt path. Mental scripts are habitual knowledge – the habits of mind which dictate our routines and typical responses to our environment. We employ mental scripts in all sorts of scenarios, not just in our empathic responses.

In the scenario above, I am using the theatrical meaning of script by imagining that the scene plays out according to a pre-determined sequence which incorporates dialogue and movement of the actors. However, how people respond to each other is determined, at least in part, by scripts in the sense of mental heuristics. It may be that our deputy rarely greets people she doesn't know very well when she encounters them by chance. This is her default position. However, when she sees friends socially, a different script kicks in and she comes across as warm and friendly. As director, we can interrupt the scene and change the script, but as a leader, we cannot rewrite the mental scripts of others so easily. We might want our deputy to be the sort of person who starts up a conversation in the car park with new staff, but we cannot implant a new script in her head.

Cultural scripts

When I visit schools, I notice people following different scripts. How people greet each other is a striking example. In the school I currently work in, I was taken aback, upon first visiting, by how many people (students and staff) would make eye contact and greet each other in a

170

friendly manner. Yet I have been to schools where staff won't even say hello to each other when they pass in the corridor. It is almost as if micro-scripts have been placed in the minds of everyone as they become part of the school community.

Mental scripts become cultural scripts when they are followed most of the time by most people in the organisation. Organisational culture is often defined as 'the way we do things around here' for this reason the people within the organisation will, to some degree, synchronise their habitual behaviours. The mental scripts we create appear to be highly influenced by the cultural norms of the organisation to which we belong; this makes sense, from an evolutionary perspective, as it is beneficial for us to 'fit in' with the group.

If we are part of the culture, we are unlikely to notice these scripts – that is, until they are broken[1]. Breaking cultural scripts can be a useful device to help change behaviour and expectations. For example, when a student hands a teacher their report card, which they have been placed on for poor behaviour, the teacher might immediately sign it to say that the student has behaved (before the lesson has even begun) and hand it back. When the student questions the teacher about their unusual behaviour, the teacher replies, 'I know you are going to behave in my lesson, you always do'. Used sparingly, and with the right student, this works.

In schools, cultural scripts will determine how students move between lessons; the way a student is talked to when they break a rule; how a difficult conversation is held between members of staff; whether the cups get washed up in the staffroom; how students enter assembly; how quickly the car park empties at the end of the day; how long staff meetings last; who gets to talk in meetings; whether teachers come into school during the holidays; how many clubs are available for students; whether staff ever get to talk to the headteacher without an appointment; whether students hold doors open for others; how uniform infringements are dealt with... almost everything you can think of that happens in a school will follow a script. If only school leaders could influence cultural scripts, they would be the directors of the school's success.

Memes contain the genetic code of school culture

To bring together the idea of a mental script and a cultural *script*, we'll define script as 'the way a scenario plays out'. A mental script determines an individual's expectations, and therefore behaviour, as a familiar situation unfolds. A cultural script is followed where the mental scripts of the players are similar due to their shared experience as members of the organisation; they have the same expectations and mental sequence for how events will unfold. School leaders should observe the scripts that those in the organisation follow – they must be students of their school's social system. Particularly interesting are the moments which capture the essence of the culture, which are called cultural *memes*. Organisational culture is *fractal*, in that each interaction mirrors the characteristics at a whole-school level (like a snowflake). Memes capture the genetic code of the organisation's culture; observe the memes and you understand better the 'ways things are done'.

To illustrate cultural memes, consider how the following scenario may play out in your school, or a school you have visited recently.

A teacher stops a student in the corridor as they are being too boisterous. Do they:

- Raise their voice at the student, chastising them publicly for their behaviour, or;

- Make eye contact as they pass and politely ask the student to quieten down, or;

- Stop the student and ask them to step to one side for a quiet word about their behaviour?

One of the above options may capture how such an incident would most commonly be dealt with by staff at the school you are picturing, or you may imagine a different script. Alternatively, you may be thinking that it would depend on who the member of staff is – there is no cultural script in this case. Your response tells us something about culture in the school. For example, in some schools, raised voices are common and staff will consider it to be quite normal that students be shouted at when they misbehave. In another school, a raised voice will be a rare exception. If there is no consistent cultural script, then that aspect of the culture is 'loose' and individuals' mental scripts are not aligned; the actors are improvising.

Look back at the list of cultural scripts listed and consider how strong the memes are in each case i.e. to what extent is there a common script which determines how scenarios play out? Perhaps imagine students entering assembly: is there a cultural expectation that they all follow (like entering in silence)? There may be rules in place which set out expectations for student behaviour; but a rule becomes a script when the majority of students follow it without thinking or prompting – in other words, what started out as a rule has been internalised by its audience. What cultural memes exist and what do they tell you about the culture across the school?

Rewriting scripts

It has been suggested that an individual's mental script is influenced by their beliefs. A belief is a mental resource which is given value and prioritised, enabling us to make decisions in complex and ill-defined situations. Leaders have a belief system: a schema which includes beliefs about what schools are for; what goals are worthy of being achieved; and what their individual role is within the school. A school leader given the brief to promote good behaviour will internalise this identity and believe that they must act in a certain way as a result; for example, by being 'tough on discipline'. This theory makes intuitive sense. However, the empirical evidence to support this is not consistent.[2]

An alternative perspective on how mental scripts come about is that behaviour is copied; in other words, cultural memes are passed from one person to the next. Copying behaviour is a sensible mental strategy as we are constantly looking for viable solutions to the problems we face. If we observe others acting in a particular way in a specific scenario with success, then we can mimic this behaviour as a short-cut to achieving desirable outcomes. This is much more efficient, and less risky, than a trial-and-error approach, which will likely see numerous failures before a successful strategy is found. Copying scripts seems likely to increase your belief that you will be successful, and following the script with success will increase this belief further. This particular type of belief, known as self-efficacy, does appear to correlate strongly with success

– in most situations being a better predictor of a positive outcome than knowledge or personality, for example. Self-efficacy reflects a confidence by the individual in their own strategic assessment of the situation at hand. The surer they are that the selected strategy will be successful, the more successful they are likely to be.

Self-efficacy is, therefore, mostly derived from observing the success of the behaviour of others (vicarious experience) and experiencing success by enacting the script successfully oneself (enactive mastery experience). To a lesser extent, encouragement by others will be of benefit, and self-efficacy will be diminished by tiredness, illness or stress. Self-efficacy is domain-specific, in that a belief that you will achieve success will be connected to the specific script you are following.[3]

Social cognitive theory[4], as the cultural-transmission ideas above are known, offers leaders an insight into how the norms of behaviour are established in schools. Leaders cannot control what others observe and mimic, but they can model cultural scripts themselves and create the conditions within which others will mimic this behaviour. Followers will be most likely to copy leaders' behaviour where:

- They observe a leader's behaviour resulting in success;
- They are able to observe other leaders also achieve success by following similar cultural scripts;
- They are physically and psychologically healthy;
- They are encouraged to model similar behaviours;
- They experience success as a result of mimicking cultural scripts.

As self-efficacy cannot be easily transferred between domains (or scripts), individuals will develop competence and confidence in each cultural script separately. As a novice in a particular script, they will think carefully about their actions and be conscious of following the script. As they become more experienced, they will habitualise the script and make it part of their routine. A useful way to think of this is to return to our theatrical analogy. To begin with, actors will read from the script in rehearsals, with the result being that the scene is stilted and artificial. However, as they memorise the script, their words and actions become automated, with the effect that the scene becomes fluid and natural.

If school leaders understand the importance of scripts and cultural transmission, they can be more deliberate in their modelling of desired behaviours. I would advocate leadership teams spending time analysing the cultural scripts they observe and, where necessary, rewriting these together so that the whole team models a consistent approach to the common scenarios that play out around the school. School leaders may also watch out for those that are regularly 'off script', acting in counter-cultural ways, and consider how such outliers can become more part of the core culture in the school, or play a role in changing scripts. As the directors of the play that is a typical school day, school leaders can begin to influence how each scene plays out.

Stage management

Modelling the desired cultural scripts is not the only way leaders can influence school culture. Leaders can more overtly script events which are of a formal nature, such as performance management meetings or lesson observations, by providing a template to complete, or questions to form the basis of discussion. These 'rules' will initially be followed clumsily but should, over time, affect the mental and cultural scripts of the participants. For example, in lesson observations, a script which requires observer and teacher to meet prior to the observation to discuss the teacher's plans and expectations for the lesson will subtly shift the subsequent discussion from one where the observer gives their views on the success of the lesson to one where they begin to ask whether the teacher achieved what they set out to. Along with some prompt questions, the tone and focus of observations can be changed from judgemental to developmental.

Overt scripting of routine staff encounters is very similar to the rules schools invent for students to follow, such as the assembly example given previously. School leaders should think of rules as only being necessary when cultural scripts are yet to be internalised by all members of the community. In schools with excellent standards of behaviour, there are often few rules on display. This is because the students take their cues from observing others and there are strong cultural scripts which members of the community have internalised and work to. In such schools, everyone knows that you don't run in the corridor and there is no need for a sign reminding students not to. If a student does break the script, they know that they will be picked up on it (often by their peers, before a teacher even gets involved). The scripts everyone follows were more explicit and visible once, but like the actors in a play, staff and students no longer need to read from the actual script, as it has been committed to memory and become routine.

Social domain-specific leadership

All schools follow different scripts. In a sense, they are all putting on a different play, albeit in the same genre. It is interesting to speculate how far back some of the cultural scripts go. Schools hold on to reputations for being 'caring', 'academic' or 'failing'. These reputations are ingrained in the expectations of those connected to the school and acted out by students, staff and parents on a daily basis. As a leader new to a school, the historically embedded aspects of school culture become apparent very quickly. School leaders need to attune themselves to cultural signals quickly, so as not to identify themselves as too much of an outsider: a defective cell that needs to be rejected. However, where significant change is needed in a school, it may be necessary to signal counter-cultural values by breaking cultural scripts. If the previous headteacher never left their office, the new headteacher might make a point of being highly visible around the school. If the last pastoral leader gave in to parental pressure too easily, the new one may make a point of holding a firm line. Following cultural scripts can be a sign to others that you belong, whereas breaking them can signal the change that is to come. Both are useful.

Given the differing cultures of schools, 'what works' will differ between contexts. Leaders cannot simply import systems or approaches any more than they can bring with them a ready-to-use toolkit of skills. Context is King: we need to learn to lead *this* school, not just *any* school. That is not to say that school leaders do not face similar problems in different schools; they do. However, the solutions to problems will differ across schools and the savvy leader will become knowledgeable in the social context, using this knowledge to help select culturally-appropriate solutions.

Summary of chapter substance

■■■■■■■ **Substance (stuff)** What do we need to know?	Scripts determine the way scenarios play out in schools. Individuals have mental scripts which influence their behaviour. When these scripts are shared, they become cultural 'ways of doing things'.
■■■■■■■ **Substance (significance)** Why is this important?	Leaders can observe the cultural scripts and act to change these by modelling or explicitly re-scripting the ways people interact and act in given situations.
■■■■■■■ **Substance (validity)** How do we know it to be true?	Social cognitive theory is a well-established field of research which studies the relationship between self and social-self.

References

1. Stigler, J. and Hiebert, J. (1999) *The Teaching Gap*. London: Simon & Schuster.

2. Watson, S. (2016) 'Teachers' Beliefs About Teaching and Learning: Their Influence on Practice', *Steven Watson* [Online], 15 January. Retrieved from: www.bit.ly/2OrX93W

3. Lunenburg, F. C. (2011) 'Self-Efficacy in the Workplace: Implications for Motivation and Performance', *International Journal of Management, Business and Administration* 14 (1).

4. Watson, S. (2016) Social Cognitive Theory, *Steven Watson* [Online], August 23. Retrieved from: www.bit.ly/2LTtgrC

Chapter 14
Indicators of change

I used to work with a particularly charismatic subject leader who was outspoken on a range of issues. He spoke in the Queen's English, despite being a boy from the valleys of Wales, and liked to make grand pronouncements whenever someone in a position of authority came near; usually about the futility of school policy. We would have lunch together in the school canteen quite often. To give you a flavour of his personality, I will share an anecdote. The dining hall was particularly noisy one day and it was becoming difficult to hold down a conversation. All of a sudden, this individual leapt to his feet and said in a very loud, clipped voice, 'On the authority of the deputy head teacher, I demand quiet!'. The hall fell into silence as the students looked from him to me (the deputy head in whose name they had been asked to quieten down). I nodded sagely as if in complete agreement, despite my bewilderment.

One of this subject leader's favourite ways of trying to annoy the school's leadership team was to say loudly, 'Here comes a senior leader to *drive up standards!*', whenever one of us approached. I never took the bait and gave as good as I got, and we ended up getting on very well. While many school leaders find people like this hard to deal with, I gravitate towards them. There is truth in their bilious wit.

'Driving up standards' is a horrible phrase, but one used by many leaders. It is symptomatic of a culture in education which places school leaders in the position of endlessly questioning whether the outcomes for students are good enough. Of course, they rarely are, and if the school is in the fortunate position of being near the top of the league tables, they will be petrified of dropping down. The relentless pressure to improve compels school leaders to identify which aspects of the school's provision are not strong enough. We 'monitor' standards, carry out audits, require self-evaluation, complete 360 degree appraisals, scrutinise student books and draw up lesson observation schedules. The language of improvement reveals how we have come to view leaders: as auditors, enforcers and 'drivers' of outcomes.

Heavy accountability systems are the result of this culture.[1] Accountability is an important concept in state schools because we are funded by the taxpayer and have a duty to ensure that every penny is well-spent. We also serve society and have a moral duty to educate future generations well. Most immediately, and what really gets most of us out of bed in the morning, we have a duty to the children in our schools, and their families. Being held to account, and holding others to account, is a necessary and desirable feature of the education system. However, accountability must be based on something of substance, lest it become corrupt and overwhelming. What we are held to account for must be meaningful, tangible and worthwhile.

I would like to soften the language around school improvement to reduce the temptation to adopt macho leadership practices. Rather than *monitoring standards* and *measuring improvement*, I propose we think in terms of *indicators of change*. School leaders must know their schools well; they should become students of their context. However, they must avoid the trap of the generic and simplistic. As we discovered in Chapter 9, schools are complex, evolving, loosely-linked organisations; change is messy, not linear, and causal relationships are unclear. We cannot measure all we see, and should not value only what we can measure. Leadership expertise means learning to sense when something is wrong, intuit dissonance, recognise progress and keep an ear to the ground.

How do we know if things are getting better?

If we strip away all the management flannel around the monitoring of standards, we are left with a simple question: are things getting better, worse, or staying the same?

The 'things' in question are similar for all schools. They include the progress of students in their learning, the quality of teaching, student behaviour and the ethos of the school. Leaders should consider what will indicate to them if these things are changing, and changing for the better. This is easier said than done. Firstly, we have to accept that it is often very difficult to say for certain whether things are changing, as the changes may be subtle, misleading or invisible to the observer (e.g. learning). Secondly, there are often observer effects i.e. the act of observing affects the subject of the observation (e.g. observing teaching). Thirdly, the inferences made from information may be unreliable and invalid (e.g. from assessment data). Fourthly, we may not know what 'better' looks like, or there may be differing views on how quality is defined (e.g. does an increase in exclusions indicate higher standards or worsening behaviour?). Lastly, in creating opportunities for leaders to know whether things are changing, there may be unintended consequences (e.g. workload).

Given the difficulties for leaders in knowing whether the school is changing in the desired ways, they must learn to cope with ambiguity, uncertainty and approximations. We often expect our leaders to be decisive, certain and in control, and it is tempting for schools to adopt simplistic, generalised systems and measures to provide a (false) impression of strength and omniscience. Such is the draw of the generic. However, if we are prepared to lead with humility and reservation, we are more likely to gain a nuanced understanding of the direction of change in our school.

Are students learning?

This is perhaps the most important question for school leaders in understanding whether children are benefiting from their education, and a whole industry has been created around providing indicators of learning. Unfortunately, it is incredibly difficult to determine whether learning has taken place, as it happens inside the student's head. The best we can hope for is a proxy for learning, which is what the student can do following a period of teaching.[2] For example, they may be able to answer a question, produce a piece of work, or perform well in an examination. Many of these proxies are highly unreliable indicators of learning. A student's ability to answer a question posed by a teacher may show that they have been listening and can regurgitate what they have been told, or it may show that information has been retained but not understood. A completed task may indicate that the student has retained knowledge in the short term, but not that they will be able to perform in the same way in a year's time. An improved piece of work may indicate that the student can act on feedback given, but may not have an understanding of why the improved work is superior to that previously produced. Many attempts to measure learning by school leaders have been crass, including lesson observations which 'evidence' students making 'rapid progress', and work scrutiny where the standard of work is taken as a reliable indicator that there has been a permanent change in the knowledge and skill of the student.[3] Over longer periods of time, school leaders have attempted to measure the learning of students as progress between two assessment points. This has often either been based on a view that students develop generic skills which they can apply across different domains of knowledge (as was the basis for National Curriculum levels), or worse, that progress can be measured according to a change in the grade achieved on tests which do not assess the same domain of knowledge. The most pernicious form of grade measurement is the flight path, which assumes that students move step by step towards the achievement of a GCSE grade.[4] It is not the place of this book to provide a full critique of the misguided attempts by educators to measure learning, but I offer the above as a warning to school leaders. If we don't fully understand how learning takes place, or carefully think through which indicators of change we choose to rely on, we will be grossly negligent and risk great harm to our schools.

Perhaps the most reliable indicator of change for learning is a well-designed, summative assessment. The benefit of a summative assessment is that it can sample from a wide domain of knowledge, acquired over an extended period of time, therefore providing a reasonably reliable indicator that students have retained a broad understanding of the curriculum taught to them. For such an assessment to be worthwhile, it must be designed carefully and carried out in controlled conditions. The assessment will need to sample proportionately from across the domain being assessed, be both accessible to those who have learnt the least and challenging for those who have learnt the most, minimise 'noise' introduced by poorly designed questions, avoid cultural bias, and result in a normally distributed spread of attainment. To ensure that valid inferences from the results can be made, the teachers should not be aware of the content of the test, students should undertake little preparation (so that the test genuinely assesses their long-term recall), sit the test at the same time and in the same conditions, and the papers should be marked blind. These requirements place significant burdens on schools, but there is little point making students sit formal tests unless the school can be confident that the results are meaningful and reliable. School leaders must develop expertise in assessment and pay attention to getting this right, which is possible if they spend less time on unreliable indicators of learning and managing systems which collate junk data.[5]

How well are teachers teaching?

It is time we accepted that we cannot tell how well teachers are teaching by simply watching them. We do not know enough about what effective teaching looks like, or if there are consistent features which will be effective in different contexts. The relationship between the teacher's actions and the students' learning is complex and unclear, and it is not possible to isolate the teacher's impact from other influences that affect student engagement and ability to learn. Furthermore, as learning is invisible and short-term proxies are highly unreliable, we cannot form judgements based on whether students learn the material taught in a lesson. The unreliability of judging teaching quality is shown in the evidence of observation inconsistency, whereby two observers will often reach very different conclusions about the effectiveness of teaching (and who is to say that either is correct?).[6]

The use of assessment data to infer teacher quality is also highly problematic. As with observation, it is difficult to separate teacher effects from student effects (such as background, interest in the subject, group mix, or personal circumstances). Assessment data has a margin of error and the small cohort size attributable to an individual teacher makes statistical inference weak. Apparent teacher effectiveness as measured through value-added scores, for instance, is also highly context dependent. Teachers are more likely to achieve lower value-added scores if they are in a department which performs less well. It is not possible to determine whether the department's performance is due to the weakness of the teachers, or the other way around. Equally, the results achieved by a teacher's class will be dependent on the performance of the school as a whole. These effects mean that you might take what appears to be a 'low performing' teacher and place them in a different department, in a different school, and suddenly see their impact on achievement significantly increase.[7]

Despite there being no reliable indicators for how effective a teacher is overall, it is possible for leaders to gain insight into some aspects of teaching practice. One aspect often missing from observation processes is an opportunity to establish the teacher's intent i.e. what they want the students to learn about and how (given their knowledge of the class) they intend to teach to maximise the likelihood that students will understand and retain what is taught. Asking about intent is important, as it provides the leader with an insight into the expectations of the teacher, their grasp of the curriculum, their knowledge of the students in the class, and how deliberately they set about the instructional process. Returning to the intent after an observation helps establish how accurately and honestly the teacher reflects on the success of the lesson (or sequence of lessons), which provides the leader with information about the teacher's capacity for self-improvement.

School leaders might also gain a sense of how teaching is changing by involving themselves directly in the process of developing teaching practice. Given that we are yet to develop a full understanding of what constitutes effective teaching, teacher development should be based on the 'best bets'. In other words, the practices we are believe will bring about better learning in the long term. One such 'best bet' is that teachers develop techniques for checking understanding and then use this information to adapt their teaching. School leaders should work with teachers to develop expertise in this aspect of their pedagogy, thereby witnessing for themselves the changes in practice. As teachers receive better feedback on the impact of their teaching and gain expertise in responding quickly and effectively to address gaps in knowledge and correct misconceptions, we can be assured that the probability that students understand will increase. If this is accompanied by frequent retrieval practice and attempts to ensure that knowledge has been retained over the longer term, then this should be reflected in the outcomes of student assessments. Knowing that teachers are changing in desirable ways and possess intentionality and reflectiveness in their thinking should give school leaders confidence that the quality of teaching is improving. It is, perhaps, the best we can hope for. We cannot *prove* that teaching standards are improving, or measure this through the application of a metric, but we can immerse ourselves in the improvement efforts and feel how strongly the current sweeps us along.

Change from whose perspective?

It wasn't so long ago that we would judge the success of a class or subject at GCSE according to how many students achieved a grade C or above. We would be pleased if this number exceeded our expectations (expectations set by national data sets). This attempt to measure success resulted in all sorts of distortions in schools. Those students on the border of a C/D grade would be the focus of intervention efforts, and performance management targets would be based around converting as many grade Ds and Es to Cs as possible. The message this gave was that those at the lower and higher ends of the grade spectrum were less important; somehow less worthy of our attention.

School leaders should be concerned about all students, but in judging whether the school is getting better, it is advisable to focus on those most vulnerable and disadvantaged. It is easy to fall into the trap of concluding that the school is improving because most students are benefiting from the changes which have taken place. The majority who benefit will most likely be the students who already have an advantage: those who can meet the higher standards expected, have experienced success in the past and feel confident that they can meet future challenges, are well supported at home, have a strong network of peer and family support, and can access the wider opportunities offered by the school. We might claim that behaviour is (generally) getting better, but is this *everyone's* behaviour? Are the most vulnerable students the remaining few who continue to get excluded? We can celebrate that results are increasing, but is this at the expense of a widening gap between the haves and have-nots?

School leaders should be particularly sensitive to whether things are improving for the most vulnerable and disadvantaged for reasons of social justice, but also for pragmatic purposes. If these students are the least likely to benefit from the changes taking place, we can judge the strength of our improvement efforts by how significantly they impact on this hard-to-reach group. This does not mean that we have to single out this group for special treatment, as is advocated by the government's pupil premium strategy, but rather that our school improvement efforts are so well designed and implemented that they impact on every child. For example, the indicator that teaching standards are improving should be that the most vulnerable and disadvantaged students learn more, not that results overall go up. These students are the main barometer of school improvement. We do not need a pupil premium strategy; we need a school improvement strategy, the success of which is based first and foremost on whether the educational outcomes for the most vulnerable and disadvantaged improve.[8]

Exam results as an indicator of change?

Naturally, school leaders will expect exam results to improve if the school delivers a better education for students. However, the measures published in school performance tables are a fairly poor proxy for school effectiveness. The Progress 8 measure is a good example. A school's Progress 8 score is calculated by comparing the grade achieved in eight subjects at GCSE with the median grade achieved in recent years in this subject by students who achieved similar SATs scores at the end of primary education. The 'value added' score is expressed as a number which represents whether, on average, students at the school achieved above or below expectations. For example, a P8 score of +0.5 means that students achieved, on average, half a grade higher than expected. The validity of the score is dependent on the accuracy of assessment, both in the KS2 SATs tests and the GCSEs, and whether each student's performance in these tests is a good indicator of their learning. Therefore, there is some statistical 'noise' in the measure. The P8 measure also only allows certain subjects and combinations of subjects to count. For example, English and maths must be included, alongside three EBacc subjects. Depending on the GCSE options chosen, it is possible for students to have empty slots in the P8 calculation. The measure takes no account of qualification difficulty, therefore assumes (wrongly) that a grade 7 in one subject is 'equivalent' to a grade 7 in another. The aggregated P8 score also takes no account of the type of students at the school, which means that a school in a disadvantaged area will have a significantly harder challenge to achieve a positive P8 score than one in an area of social advantage. The Progress 8 score is such a grossly over-simplified measure that it is meaningless to compare schools in this way.

But what might we infer from improving exam results within a school over time? Steadily increasing exam results is certainly an indicator of change, but not always of higher standards. School leaders must be sure to understand why exam results are increasing. Here are some of the reasons exam results may improve without there necessarily being any greater impact of teaching and learning:

- **Changes in cohort demographics:** Certain types of students tend to secure higher value-added scores. For example, there are wide variations between different ethnic groups. A change in the school's demographic can have a significant impact on outcomes.

- **The curriculum:** Students may have taken 'softer' qualifications which boost their average grade (such as seen by the high entry levels for the European Computer Driving Licence – ECDL – course until its removal from Progress 8 calculations in 2018). Students may also take combinations of subjects that fill all the slots in the Progress 8 calculation, perhaps as a deliberate policy by a school to ensure this is the case.

- **Extensive intervention programmes:** Schools may introduce additional lessons and individual or small group tutoring to increase outcomes. These may include after school or holiday revision programmes which strategically target 'under-achieving' students.

In our high-stakes accountability system, it is unsurprising that improved exam results can become the goal of school leaders, rather than just an indicator of higher standards. Whatever moral position we may take on this, the reality is that the ways schools respond to the pressure for better results further undermines exam performance as a reliable indicator of increasing school standards. School leaders should be honest with themselves about how results have been achieved and the extent to which they can attribute success to meaningful educational improvement. Besides which, by the time the results come out, it is too late to do anything about it.

The cranes in Dublin

According to *The Irish Times*,[9] the number of cranes in Dublin hit an all-time high in March 2019. 123 cranes towered above the Dublin skyline, indicating an unprecedented level of construction activity in Ireland's capital city.

The crane survey carried out by *The Irish Times* is an example of a *leading indicator* in economics. The idea is that the traditional *lagged indicators* used to measure the success of the economy (e.g. GDP, national income, unemployment) only tell us what has happened well after the event, and therefore are of limited pragmatic use in the short term. Approximations of economic activity, such as the number of cranes erected, which indicates how much building work is taking place, therefore the level of confidence of industry that the economy will prosper, provide a signal of change well before the official statistics are compiled.

In schools, we have come to rely on lagged indicators such as exam results, assessments taken at the end of a period of teaching, parent surveys, staff absence statistics and summary attendance data. This data is useful in knowing how well we were doing, but not how well we are doing now; neither does it warn us early enough of impending problems. Leaders should watch for leading indicators. Consider the following examples and what we might infer from each:

- The amount of litter on the field at the end of lunch.
- The number of hands raised when teachers are asking questions in class.
- The frequency of raised voices by teachers as you walk around the school.
- The amount of students who look you in the eye and say hello as they get off the bus in the morning.

- Attendance at morning briefing.
- The number of cars in the car park two hours after the end of the school day.

Schools might also prioritise collecting and analysing real-time data over lagged data, such as attendance, late marks, missed homework, rewards and sanctions. To justify the collection of such live data, the school must be geared towards responding quickly to tackle emerging problems. For example, pastoral leaders might quickly spot an increase in missed homework by a normally reliable student and enquire as to whether home circumstances have changed, or if the student is struggling with workload. Leading indicators should point towards both whole-school patterns and changes in behaviours at a granular level.

Cultural indicators

In Chapter 13, we considered the cultural memes that school leaders should be sensitive to. Evolving norms of behaviour are an important indicator of change which often foretell more concrete measures. Targeting cultural indicators may prove more effective than more abstract targets, such as measures of student progress or exam grades. For instance, a deliberate attempt to reduce lateness to lessons will increase learning time and ensure a less disruptive start. Such targets are more concrete and achievable than, say, aiming to increase the attainment of low prior attaining students. The latter will be judged successful if value-added outcomes increase for this group, whereas the former may be judged successful within days and be a leading indicator of eventual success in improving learning for tardy students.

School improvement strategies which set targets around arbitrary groups of students are also problematic. This practice is encouraged by aggregated measures of success, such as exam outcomes for pupil premium students. There are groups of students with common barriers to learning, such as those who are repeatedly late to lessons, but it is important to identify groups according to the specific behaviours which prevent their achievement rather than by their socio-economic group or prior attainment. School leaders will have greater impact if they focus on the specifics of how students engage with their education, and greater urgency is created if the indicators of change are concrete and immediate.

Open minds, not just open doors

A favourite cliché of school leaders is to tell staff that their door is always open; that may be so, but is their mind equally open? Collectively, the staff of a school know far, far more about what is going on than school leaders. They are at the frontline and will be sensitive to leading indicators of change. Without their collective wisdom, school leaders will miss many signals that the school is changing, for better or worse. To tap into this tide of data, school leaders must be genuinely open and responsive to feedback. Most importantly, when told something they don't want to hear, they must avoid being defensive and ensure that the message-bearer is thanked, not chastised. This is difficult for leaders who, like everyone else, can become overwhelmed by the challenges of their job, but it is vitally important that they adopt the mindset that all feedback is good feedback.

Not only must leaders be open to honest feedback, but they should seek it out. However approachable leaders are, many staff will not walk through their office door and report their views or observations. Even if they are happy to speak truth to power, they might not want to bother the 'busy' leader with relatively petty concerns. School leaders must have casual encounters with all staff and ask direct questions to elicit their views. Catching staff when they are on break duty is ideal for such encounters, or dropping by the staff room for a chat over a cup of coffee. Maintaining a presence around the school not only supports good student conduct and provides reassurance for staff that senior leaders are 'hands-on', but it significantly increases the likelihood that someone will pass on an observation which is an early warning sign of future problems, or perhaps even give some positive feedback which indicates that the efforts to engender change are working. Leaders that walk and listen a lot will be months ahead of the data.

As I argued in Chapter 4, to know what conditions are like on the ground, walk the terrain.[10] Abstract, aggregate, backward-looking measures will never truly reflect the messy nature of school improvement. There is no substitute for knowing the school in which you work, and this requires open eyes, ears and mind. The indicators of change are all around you and it is the leader's job to look for the signs, rather than to expect others to show you the evidence. When it comes to standards, school leaders must have their finger on the pulse, not the trigger.

Summary of chapter substance

▬▬▬▬▬▬	
Substance (stuff) What do we need to know?	School leaders must know whether, how quickly, and in what way the school is changing. However, the indicators they rely on must be valid, reliable and unobtrusive. The way leaders approach this challenge should reflect the complex and messy nature of change within schools, and quantitative, lagged indicators should not take precedence over qualitative, leading indicators.
Substance (significance) Why is this important?	Leaders' attempts to monitor standards and evidence improvement can distort organisational objectives and behaviour in a damaging way, often leading to heavy-handed accountability systems. School leaders must have their finger on the pulse, not the trigger.
Substance (validity) How do we know it to be true?	Critiques of over-blown accountability systems and simplistic measures of school success are well documented and beginning to be recognised by policy makers e.g. the DfE's report from the Workload Advisory Group and 2019 changes to the Ofsted Inspection Framework.

Further reading and references

This chapter makes few specific references to individual texts but draws broadly from a wide range of sources. I have referenced possible sources of further reading for those interested.

1. An illustration of the effect of burdensome data-collection systems in schools can be found in the DfE's Workload Advisory Group's report 'Making Data Work', which can be found here: www.bit.ly/338YZur

2. For a more detailed explanation of proxies for learning, see David Didau's blog post, found here: www.bit.ly/2MnRg55

3. For a detailed argument about the validity of using exercise books to infer progress, see my blog post on the topic here: www.bit.ly/2o9lFfr

4. For more on why flight paths are a problem, see David Didau's blog post, found here: www.bit.ly/2VjgQwd

5. A useful source of information for school leaders interested in assessment is Daisy Christodoulou's 2017 book *Making Good Progress.*

6. Strong, M., Gargani, J. and Hacifazliogluet, O. (2011) 'Do We Know a Successful Teacher When We See One? Experiments in the Identification of Successful Teachers', *Journal of Teacher Education* 62 (4) pp. 367-382.

7. For more about the preoccupation with teacher effectiveness, see my blog post on the topic here: www.bit.ly/30SCwAf

8. For more on the flaws in the pupil premium strategy, see Dr Rebecca Allen's series of blog posts on the topic, particularly this one: www.bit.ly/2NLAob1

9. Comiskey, J. (2019) 'Dublin Crane Count Reaches Record 123 in March', *The Irish Times* [Online], 6 March. Retrieved from: www.bit.ly/2pNMJ45

10. For more on the benefits of walking around the school, see my blog post on the topic here: www.bit.ly/33jVGAX

Chapter 15
Leadership in its place

In Chapter 1, I suggested that leadership may be a construct without substance; a convenient term used to describe a multitude of behaviours, theories, attributes and relationships, but one which does not hold up to close scrutiny. As we have explored the field of leadership, we have indeed found a multitude of definitions, a fair degree of rhetoric and a frequent tendency to favour the generic over the specific. In schools, leadership has often been held up as the answer to our problems, but over-reaches itself in the delivery. In the absence of clear purpose and an operating framework to guide their actions, school leaders have struggled to transform the system to secure sustained, improved outcomes for the nation's children.

However, we have also found places where leadership appears to fulfil a pragmatic purpose. Leaders may help bring clarity to solve schools' swampy problems, provide unity of purpose, galvanise the efforts of the workforce, shape cultural norms and be sensitive to the signs of change. We have discovered a place for leadership not by concerning ourselves with the leader, but with the school itself: its nature, needs and purpose. Leadership is to be found in the specific; its roots drawing sustenance from domains of knowledge and expertise. To discover something about leadership, we have turned away from it and towards the concrete reality of the enterprise of running a school. In doing so, we have moved from a position of scepticism to one of 'suspicious engagement'[1] with the concept of leadership.

Identity or mask?

It has been said that if one wants to understand what is happening in organisations, leadership is often a bad place to start.[2] It is often portrayed as sitting above the day-to-day concerns of those on the ground, or as separate and distinct from the gritty problems which arise. Leaders appear to transcend the detail, concerning themselves with the big picture and the long view. In doing so, leadership makes itself an easy target for criticism, but we can reclaim leadership if we recognise its limits and tether it back to the situationally specific.

Leadership can help us move forward, but the answer is not always to lead. In calling ourselves 'leaders', we have adopted a persona; 'leader' is our title and this is what we consider ourselves to be. However, leading is only one, arguably minor, part of what school 'leaders' do. If I think about my working week as a headteacher, how often do I lead? Significant amounts of time are taken up with anything but: with administrating, managing, prioritising, responding, supervising, reporting and reading. We have chosen our identity from one of many possible roles we play and, in doing so, have elevated leadership in importance above all else. We have rejected the title of manager as too mundane; leader sounds so much more dynamic!

And what else would we call ourselves? In essence, those in 'leadership' positions are simply the accountable person – the buck stops here. Is this all that distinguishes us? Responsibility can be delegated, tasks offloaded, power given away if we choose; even our leadership can be 'distributed'. Seniority provides some locus of control in return for an acceptance that we are, ultimately, the person to whom others will pin the rosette, or the blame. Perhaps, in the end, this is all that leadership is.

Rather than defining our identity, we can choose to wear leadership as a mask when it is needed. There are times when leading is required of us, when it is the right response to the situation at hand. At these times, we should bring leadership into play by demonstrating moral purpose, rallying the troops, cutting through uncertainty and securing victory. At other times we may remove the mask and bring something else: the prudent financial manager, meticulous administrator, critical friend, supportive colleague or technical expert. Leader is not who we are, just one of the things we do. We should question when leadership is useful, when it is not, what type of leadership is required and for how long, and how strong the intervention should be. Leadership should be seen as temporal and situation specific, rather than permanently defining relations between those in the organisation.[3]

Leadership is also not the only organisational paradigm – believe it or not, things can improve without leaders. Professional autonomy may be preferable in organisations where educated, morally motivated individuals impact significantly on achieving successful outcomes. The central importance of knowledge and expertise in schools make them particularly suitable for forms of organisation which allow significant freedoms in decision-making. Professionals may also naturally tend towards working in communities of practice; for example, gravitating towards other experts in their subject domain, regardless of the formal hierarchical requirement to do so. Where some conformity and centralisation is needed, democratic structures might also serve a useful purpose. Collective decision-making is a viable alternative to centralised managerial control where there is a need for consensus and high levels of buy-in. Even bureaucracy, a much-maligned term which brings to mind endless form-filling, has a role to play in ensuring that organisations operate efficiently. Leaders must be mindful that their leadership can have a crowding-out effect on other ways of being. In short, leadership should be kept in its place. This quote from Alvesson and Spicer summarises the position well:

> Leadership could thus be seen as a productive and communicatively grounded asymmetry in work relations, invoked in situations where co-ordination, mutual adjustments, bureaucracy (rules), professionalism and other means of control do not work well. Such deliberation would clarify when leadership could be evoked and when it might not be. Rather than the leader leading people most of the time, one could imagine that autonomy and supportive horizontal relations in combination with organisational structures and cultural meanings and norms take care of most things at work, but that occasionally leadership may be necessary or positive.[4]

The object of leadership

School leaders must also be careful to direct their leadership towards the right objects. In Chapter 10, I argued that too little attention has been paid to *what* is being taught in schools in recent times. Schools have instead focused on the functional aspects of teaching and learning, but in the absence of disciplinary understanding, have created what Christine Counsell called an 'intransitive pedagogy – a pedagogy without object'.[5] When leaders focus relentlessly on improving a particular aspect of school performance, they can have great impact. But if the object is poorly chosen, the result can be damaging, and a distraction from meaningful school improvement.

The choice of goal and measure of success are also significant in ensuring that leadership has a constructive focus. In Chapter 14, I argued that the pursuit of simplistic, unreliable indicators of success, such as examination outcomes or teacher effectiveness, misdirect efforts which would be more productively focused on specific, more immediate objectives: creating a positive culture, improving standards of behaviour, ensuring reliable assessments and helping teachers get better. Leadership is a scarce resource and it should be deployed towards meaningful and achievable aims.

School leaders should also avoid fanciful notions. In Chapter 12, I critiqued the grand visions of leaders, designed to compel others to dream the impossible dream. Such ambitions may look good on the school website but are removed from the daily reality of hard-working, committed professionals. Leaders should portray a simple, moral purpose in all that they do, and seek to influence, rather than control, by winning the trust and respect of those who will deliver educational quality. Leaders do not need mystical qualities, such as emotional intelligence, to secure the allegiance of their followers. They simply need to exercise their natural human tendencies to be respectful, personable and kind. The school should be the object of the leader's attention, not their own status or ability.

A healthy suspicion of leadership teaches us to employ it conservatively, direct it cautiously and keep it in its place.

Leading with substance

I stated, in the Introduction, that this is not a handbook. However, as we near the end of Section 2, I feel the need to provide some vignettes which might be returned to as an aide-memoire and guide the reader in the application of the principles outlined in this book. In the style of Spinal Tap, I have ramped this list up to 11 for extra effect.

1. **Be a student of your school.** Come to know its people, ethos, foibles, peculiarities, cultural norms, hidden places, dark secrets, harboured dreams, storage cupboards, social dynamics, potted history, defining moments, reputation, uniqueness and dullness. Let your leadership grow in the rich soil of the school.

2. **Expand your knowledge.** Read widely. Walk the school every day. Cherish chance encounters. Listen. No, really listen... and try to understand. Visit other schools and talk to people in them. Read more.

3. **Solve problems.** Develop expertise in solving swampy problems. Keep practising and reflecting; seek feedback on your success. Get things wrong. Draw on the expertise of others. Let them make the decisions if they know more than you.

4. **Keep changing your mind.** Assume that what you believe to be true now will probably be cast in doubt when you know more. Act accordingly with humility. Seek out alternative viewpoints to your own and understand that you might be wrong. Make the best decisions you can with what you know now, and stand by them.

5. **Beware genericism.** Develop a radar which detects the simplistic, the distracting, the bullshit, the noise, the abstract, the misleading and the immoral. Resist quick-wins and looking good over being good.

6. **Be led by your values.** Know what you stand for. Portray a clear purpose in all that you do.

7. **Choose the objects of your leadership wisely.** Understand the curriculum and value disciplinary diversity. Resist measuring the unmeasurable. Direct your precious time developing others rather

than controlling them. Accept that most good things that will happen will happen without your leadership. Focus your attention on small changes, not grand gestures,

8. **Write the script and direct the play.** Notice cultural memes. Act to change those that do not reflect your values. Model the behaviours you expect of others. Tell them when they fall short of your expectations and help them do better next time. Be explicit about how you want things to be and work with your team to reset cultural norms.

9. **Seek feedback.** Have an open door, then walk through it to meet people on their territory. Treat all feedback as positive. Be sensitive to indicators of change. Accept that change is messy; look for a multitude of signals and learn to live with ambiguity.

10. **Only lead when leadership is required.** Don't overestimate your importance. Step back and think about whether leadership is the right solution to this problem. Exercise your leadership with caution. First, do no harm. Think about the substance of what you hope to achieve and do not become preoccupied with your leadership brilliance. Put leadership back in the box when you have finished with it and get on with the rest of your job.

11. **Look after yourself.** There are more important things in life than being a leader.

Having rediscovered a little of what it means to lead, we lastly turn our attention to how we can develop leadership practice and ensure that leadership substance is at the heart of our schools.

Summary of chapter substance

▬▬▬▬▬▬ **Substance (stuff)** What do we need to know?	A healthy suspicion of leadership teaches us to employ it conservatively, direct it cautiously and keep it in its place.
▬▬▬▬▬▬ **Substance (significance)** Why is this important?	Leadership can be damaging, particularly where it selects the wrong object, exceeds the limits of necessity and pursues fanciful, unworthy or unrealistic goals. However, in the right hands, at the right time, leadership is a powerful tool.

Substance (validity) How do we know it to be true?	The misguided school leader is as apt to leave a trail of destruction as they are to forge a path to success.

References

1. Alvesson M. and Spicer, A. (2012) *Critical Leadership Studies: The Case for Critical Performativity*. The Tavistock Institute. Thousand Oaks, CA: Sage Publishing.

2. Pfeffer, J. (1977) 'The Ambiguity of Leadership', *Academy of Management Review* 2 (1) pp. 104-112.

3. Sveningsson, S. and Larsson, M. (2006) 'Fantasies of Leadership: Identity Work', *Leadership* 2 (2) pp. 203-224.

4. Alvesson M. and Spicer, A. (2012) *Critical Leadership Studies: The Case for Critical Performativity*. The Tavistock Institute. Thousand Oaks, CA: Sage Publishing.

5. Counsell, C. (2016) 'Genericism's children', *The dignity of the thing* [Online], 11 January. Retrieved from: www.bit.ly/337CDJQ

Section 3
Substantially Better Leadership

Chapter 16
Our leadership inheritance

Unconscious incompetence

If we are to become better leaders, we should start with an honest appraisal of how well we lead. After all, we cannot hope to develop our competence if we do not identify where it is currently lacking. Tragically, it would appear that we are unlikely to make an accurate assessment of just how good, or bad, we are.

In 1999, Justin Kruger and David Dunning of Cornell University set out why we find it so difficult to make an accurate assessment of our own abilities across a range of fields in a paper titled 'Unskilled and Unaware of It: How Difficulties in Recognizing One's Own Incompetence Lead to Inflated Self-Assessments'.[1] Kruger and Dunning demonstrated that people tend to overestimate their abilities in many social and intellectual pursuits; particularly if they are not very competent. The main reason for this misjudgement was the same as the reason for their incompetence: namely a lack of knowledge. Their inability to do a task well also means that they do not possess the insight to realise what it is they are getting so wrong. In fact, they often don't even realise they are performing incompetently, such is their ignorance. This phenomenon has since been known as the Dunning-Kruger Effect, and can be found across many domains where success depends on knowledge and expertise.

How can it be that incompetent people do not begin to realise that the repeated failures they experience are a result of their ineffectiveness?

One possibility is that they do not receive negative feedback on their efforts, which in a work context may well be true, as most people will avoid telling someone that they are deficient in some way. However, even if people do receive negative feedback, they may attribute failure not to their own mistakes but to factors outside of their control. Kruger and Dunning put it thus:

> The problem with failure is that it is subject to more attributional ambiguity than success. For success to occur, many things must go right: the person must be skilled, apply effort, and perhaps be a bit lucky. For failure to occur, the lack of any one of these components is sufficient. Because of this, even if people receive feedback that points to a lack of skill, they may attribute it to some other factor.

Incompetent individuals are also unable to recognise competence when they see it and make favourable or unfavourable comparisons between themselves and others. In sum, incompetent individuals will be lacking negative feedback, attribute failure to factors beyond their control, and be unable to identify qualities in others which they lack themselves.

Highly competent individuals also seem to suffer from a bias in self-assessment of their abilities, but in the opposite direction. While more competent people do possess the knowledge to know when things have gone well, they tend to assume that others must be performing equally well. It is as if, when success is so commonly experienced, one assumes that it is more widespread than is actually the case. High performing individuals thereby assess their absolute abilities quite accurately, but not their relative performance.

Collective delusion

The work of Kruger, Dunning and others in the field of self-assessment shows that the majority of us will assess our abilities as above average in most domains. This should make us at least a little paranoid as leaders. If we think we are quite good at leading, are we among those who don't realise just how good we are, or those who grossly underestimate our incompetence?

But what if the over-estimation of our true ability is not limited to under-performing individuals, but endemic across the domain of leadership? What if we are collectively ignorant of just how bad we are?

A core contention of this book is that many of our leadership constructs are misleading, therefore we do not have reliable criteria against which to assess leadership effectiveness. Any attempt to rate our generic leadership skills will be fruitless if we find, as I have asserted, that there are no such things. We might develop sophisticated tools for evaluating a leader's emotional intelligence, for example, but if our construct is flawed, then the score we award ourselves will be meaningless. Comparing ourselves to the latest fashionable 'theory of everything', such as transformational leadership, will also be unlikely to provide a consistent benchmark for measuring our effectiveness. The deficiencies in our understanding of leadership mean that we search in the wrong places, idolise false gods and take dead-end paths. The evidence of our delusion is in the consistent debunking of theory, the speed with which today's heroes fall into disrepute and the fragility of many successful 'turnaround' schools which decline once more. If we really understood leadership, surely we would have been more fruitful in deploying it with success across our system?

Our collective ignorance about leadership could be the fundamental barrier to individual improvement. Until we have a valid and accurate conceptualisation of leadership, we have nothing reliable against which to compare ourselves. The raw materials for a breakthrough in our understanding are available. There is evidence about which leadership actions have impact, but these scraps of knowledge lack a coherent paradigm to give them meaning. Like all leaps forward in human endeavour, we just need to see what we already know in a different way.

Geocentric leadership

Over two thousand years ago, scholars began to question the view that the Earth rested at the centre of the universe and that everything else revolved around it. However, geocentrism (as this is known) continued to be the generally accepted view until the turn of the 16th century, when Nicolaus Copernicus developed a mathematical model for a heliocentric view in which all celestial bodies rotated around the Sun. The Copernican Revolution, as it became known, lasted for around one hundred years, until Sir Isaac Newton's observations provided the first solid proof of the heliocentric model. This paradigm shift meant that the observational data collected up until this point suddenly (if you can call a period of one hundred years 'sudden') made sense. For example, the observed data showing the movement of Mars in relation to the Earth appeared to plot a bizarre orbit in the geocentric model, with Mars performing a little loop at a point in its orbit. The observations of the relative movement of these two bodies was not incorrect, but the paradigm which gave meaning to these observations was. The same data, once a heliocentric model was assumed, showed Mars making an elliptical orbit around the Sun in the same manner as the Earth. This paradigm shift made way for others to define the laws of gravity and motion at a universal scale. The elliptical orbit of Mars around the Sun, rather than the Earth, not only made sense of the observational data, but in relation to the theories and proofs which came later. Rather than the data creating confusion, the paradigm shift allowed the data to take us one step closer to the truth. In other words, humans were able to perceive what they already 'knew' in a different way, and this different way allowed lots of parts of the jigsaw to begin to fit together.

What if we are stuck in our own geocentric leadership paradigm, assuming that so much revolves around the leader? If this were the case, then the observational data we have collected on leadership is not necessarily wrong, it is just that we cannot make sense of it by applying our current paradigm.

Let's explore this hypothesis with an example. In Chapter 5, we discussed the popular theory of 'transformational leadership'. Like so many conceptions of leadership, this theory places the leader at the centre of school improvement efforts: as the catalyst and driver for substantial change to the organisation. In descriptions of such leaders, everything appears to rotate around the leader, as if they are the centre of gravity. Their charisma pulls people towards them; their ability to inspire creates a whirlwind of motion and energy. Without the leader, we would be left drifting in space and time. This model assumes that the leader's importance 'outweighs' that of the school itself. When you perceive the leader as the central point around which everything else orbits, you will interpret your observations accordingly. Data which shows that things are improving for the school will be attributed to the force of the leader. The behaviours of those who change the organisation will not be credited to their own agency and effort, but to the catalysing charisma of the leader: the supposed centre of mass.

If we were to remove the leader as the central focus, how might we begin to interpret the data? For example, by placing the school at the centre of our paradigm, relegating the leader to an orbiting body, how do we adjust our perspective? There is no doubt that the leader has gravity – exerting some influence on the other celestial bodies – but there is an interplay with much greater forces, such as the momentum of the school's journey through space and time. Transformational leaders may temporarily pull the school off its current trajectory, but when they are removed, there are greater forces which determine the school's likely future. We might conceive of transformational leaders more like an asteroid; temporarily entering our solar system and disrupting the objects within it, before disappearing into the vast, empty void.

My contention is simply that the paradigm matters. When we place the leader at the centre of our view of school improvement, when we pay it too much attention and award it too much importance, it distorts our interpretation of what is actually happening. The data we collect might be accurate, but we could be interpreting it in the wrong way. In relation to judging how effective we are as school leaders, there is a good chance we are suffering from a mass delusion – a sort of collective Dunning-Kruger Effect whereby, as a group, we are judging our effectiveness in ignorance of what good leadership actually looks like.

Collective intelligence

In Chapter 3, I asked whether we need clever leaders. My conclusion was that we probably do, but that a notion of general intelligence places insufficient weight on the domain-specific knowledge that expert leaders must possess to be effective. However, if we have a false conception of leadership, we may be employing our individual intelligence in ineffective ways – cleverly doing the wrong things. As leaders, we are entirely dependent on the collective knowledge of those who have come before us, on our cultural inheritance.

Enter Thomas Thwaites, a post-graduate design student at the Royal College of Arts in London. Thwaites is the man who tried to build a toaster. Thwaites's story came to my attention thanks to the economist Tim Harford and succinctly sums up just how much each of us relies on the inherited culture of our species.[2]

Thwaites didn't just try to build a toaster from the available components, or even raw materials. He went back to the beginning, sourcing materials himself and manufacturing every part of the toaster. He sourced iron from a mine in Wales and obtained copper by electrolysis of polluted water. He soon found that his goal would not be possible without a few cheats: melting down commemorative coins to get nickel and finding plastic in his local dump, rather than extracting the oil from the earth itself. Nonetheless, wherever he could, Thwaites stayed true to his mission of building a toaster with as little assistance from the economic infrastructure of the modern world as possible. Harford notes that a toaster has more than 400 components and is made from nearly 100 different materials. To achieve Thwaites's vision would have taken a lifetime, yet such a machine is available from your local Argos for £9.99.

Thwaites completed his toaster. In the end, it never quite toasted, but it warmed a piece of bread quite well. That was until he plugged it into the mains supply, when it melted.

The toaster story is an allegory for the complexity of our modern economy, which either leaves us in wonder at the power of the global efforts and knowledge to deliver such technology into our hands, or despair at the vast industrialisation which is out of human control and threatens to destroy the planet on which we live. Either way, it exemplifies the fact that our individual knowledge is insignificant compared to the collective intelligence of hundreds of generations which came before us. We either stand on the shoulders of giants, or on the shoulders of fools, depending on how you choose to see it.

So, we are only as smart as our culture. Even those we hold up as geniuses can only extend human knowledge marginally from its current position and cannot make intuitive leaps far beyond the boundaries of the accumulated understanding of their age. Newton was able to collect the data to support Copernicus' model of the solar system, but he was unable to comprehend the idea that matter bends and slows time.[3] Few of us can claim to have the profound insight of those who have added so significantly to collective human understanding, but all of us have access to more knowledge than these intellectual heavyweights. As the writer Matt Ridley said: 'I cannot hope to match [Adam] Smith's genius as an individual, but I have one great advantage over him – I can read his book.'[4]

As school leaders, our individual intelligence and ability is little compared to our inherited knowledge of the domain of school leadership. We are not building a toaster from scratch. If we wish to improve leadership across the school system, we can nurture individual leaders, but we must also build our cultural inheritance: our collective knowledge of how schools improve, and what role leadership has to play. The Copernican Revolution cautions us to question the paradigm through which we make sense of the evidence. Our observations may be accurate, but how we make sense of the data may be creating confusion rather than insight. We will only move forward if we interpret our inherited wisdom with care.

Becoming a better leader

At the start of this chapter, I asserted that if we are to become better leaders, we must firstly make an honest assessment of how well we lead. This has been shown to be problematic, both individually and collectively. Not only are we often a poor judge of our own competence, but we may also be suffering from a collective delusion about the nature and importance of leadership. Enlightenment will only come if we engage critically with our assumptions about leadership. We need to develop a better understanding of what role leadership plays in school improvement, and what good leadership looks like. Leaders must have access to a reliable cultural inheritance which accurately defines and explains leadership. Only then will they begin to make informed judgements about their competence as a leader and begin the journey of self-improvement.

Summary of chapter substance

■■■■■■■■ **Substance (stuff)** What do we need to know?	Our judgement about how effective we are as leaders is probably inaccurate. At an individual level, we are unaware of our incompetence and underestimate our competence. Our knowledge of the nature and importance of leadership is unreliable; therefore, we do not really know how good (or bad) we collectively are as school leaders. We must critically engage with our assumptions about leadership to ensure that we stand on the shoulders of giants, not fools.
■■■■■■■■ **Substance (significance)** Why is this important?	Becoming consciously aware of our competence or incompetence is the first step to improving our effectiveness as leaders.
■■■■■■■ **Substance (validity)** How do we know it to be true?	The Dunning-Kruger Effect is a well-established phenomenon. The evidence of our collective delusion about leadership is in the consistent debunking of theory, the speed with which today's heroes fall into disrepute, and the fragility of many successful 'turnaround' schools which decline once more.

References

1. Kruger, J. and Dunning, D. (1999) 'Unskilled and Unaware of It: How Difficulties in Recognizing One's Own Incompetence Lead to Inflated Self-Assessments', *Journal of Personality and Social Psychology* 77 (6) pp. 1121-1134.

2. Tim Harford's article on Thomas Thwaites can be found here: www.bit.ly/1np7drw

3. Stewart-Williams, S. (2018) 'How Culture Makes Us Smarter', Psychology Today [Online], 14 December. Retrieved from: www.bit.ly/2RZ3D99

4. Sternberg, E. (2012) 'The Rational Optimist: How Prosperity Evolves' – By Matt Ridley, *Economic Affairs* 32 (2) pp. 106-107.

Chapter 17
A leadership curriculum and pedagogy

How do we develop expert leaders?

In Chapter 9, I argued that expert leaders apply domain-specific knowledge flexibly to solve complex problems. I also argued that domain-specific knowledge can be taught, but that the ability to apply this knowledge flexibly can only be learnt through practice across a wide range of contexts. How, then, might we best support leaders in moving from novice to expert practice?

One approach to educating leaders is through formal development programmes. Such programmes draw on the theory of, and research into, leadership to define a curriculum and pedagogy for developing leadership expertise. Defining the curriculum for leadership programmes is problematic. Programme designers must make decisions about what knowledge and skills to include, and how these might helpfully be defined, grouped and conceptualised. In the absence of an agreed definition of leadership, a robust theoretical framework and firm evidence of which leadership practices are effective, it is no surprise that leadership development programmes vary widely in their structure, curriculum and pedagogic approach.

Parsing problems

Any attempt to write a curriculum for leadership will have to answer the question of how to define its component parts. For example, we might divide our curriculum into topics such as strategic planning, school culture or managing people. Alternatively, we might identify specific skills to be taught, such as holding difficult conversations, setting performance targets or presentational techniques. In Chapter 2, I presented an argument which helps us understand why both of these approaches may be flawed. Firstly, to teach skills separately from the specific knowledge which the leader will draw upon to solve leadership problems will be ineffective, as skills do not exist separately from that domain knowledge. Secondly, to teach merely the knowledge required for leadership without providing opportunities for the leader to practise applying this knowledge to help solve specific problems risks, leaving the leader as a knowledgeable incompetent.

In her paper entitled 'Parsing the Practice of Teaching' in 2016, Mary Kennedy addresses a very similar problem in relation to teacher development programmes[1]. Kennedy describes the problems faced by those attempting to 'partition the fluid practice of teaching' as follows:

- **Grain size:** If teaching practice is divided into very small bits, the curriculum becomes fragmented and crowded. Too large and we lose clarity on specific practices;
- **Losing meaning:** By isolating component parts we may lose sight of the role each plays in the entirety of practice, or not be able to identify which approach is better than another;
- **Fads:** We are susceptible to fashionable ideas and disregarding those that have fallen out of favour.

These problems are illustrated through Kennedy's critique of the historical approaches which have been taken to parsing teaching practice. One such attempt, all the way back in the late 1920s, was the Commonwealth Teacher Training Study[2] which set out to identify and classify all the things that teachers do[3] so that a useful curriculum of relevant knowledge for teachers could be established. The comprehensive list of teacher actions, generated through analysis of job descriptions and surveys of teachers and others involved in education, included 1,001 items which were then sorted into seven categories. This curriculum illustrates the grain size problem, in that the items on the lists varied considerably in scale and complexity, from the 100 specific actions under the category of 'recording and reporting', to the sizeable task of 'adapting assignments to the abilities and needs of the class'. The framework did not reveal anything about the relative importance of each part, or the interdependence of the parts, thereby failing to provide a sense of how teachers might use their knowledge in pursuit of larger goals, or how these may be useful to them in a particular context.

An alternative approach to parsing teaching practice has been a more explicit focus on knowledge over practice, last fashionable in the late 1980s[4]. There was a series of attempts at the time to define increasingly large bodies of knowledge, segregated into domains. One of the contentions of this book is that domain-specific knowledge is indeed important in developing expert practice. However, the potential body of knowledge for complex, 'fluid practices' such as teaching and leadership is enormous, and the specific knowledge required by each practitioner will vary widely depending on context and goals. Furthermore, the knowledge practitioners require is not compartmentalised declarative knowledge, but a rich schema held in the mind, which is flexible, interconnected and readily available for practitioners to draw upon to perform their roles. As with the attempt to identify the actions teachers take, a purely knowledge-focused approach loses sight of meaning – what do we hold this knowledge for and how should it be applied?

Illustrating the faddish nature of parsing approaches, more recent attempts have focused on broader groups of observable behaviours, termed by some as 'core practices'[5,6]. These may include stylistic categories of teaching such as 'lecturing' or 'group work' or be defined at a subject specific level; for example, how teachers of history engage students in the study of historical sources. Parsing teaching practice in this way may be an improvement on previous approaches, as the way they are described implies value judgements about the purposes of education, and which meaningful educational endeavours students should be engaged in. For example, in science we might identify 'engaging in scientific enquiry' as a core practice. By doing so, we are indicating our belief that one purpose of the science curriculum is to introduce children to, or even inculcate them into, the traditions of practice within the wider science community. This purpose would not be universally accepted as a goal of pre-16 science education, therefore its inclusion in a curriculum for teachers would introduce a subjective position on the role of the subject and schooling more broadly. It is perhaps no surprise that there has been some resurgence of debate, particularly on social media, about 'traditional' versus 'progressive' ideology, as educators engaging in dialogue about teaching grapple with the parsing problem as they attempt to think through what it means to be an effective practitioner. The 'core practices' approach also has the benefit that the components of practice, being of sufficient scale and scope, will be relevant to most teachers for most of the time. Furthermore, it can be adapted to the particular context in which the teacher finds themselves.

Despite the apparent benefits of a 'core practices' approach to the parsing problem, Kennedy points to the tendency for novice teachers, in particular, to focus on procedural aspects of these practices and quickly lose sight of the educational goals. For example, in educating teachers about the practice of 'managing discussions', teachers can be drawn into practising techniques, such as asking students to extend their response to questions, but lose sight of the broader educational purpose, such as ensuring that all children in the class understand and retain the knowledge taught. Kennedy states that 'when we define teaching by the visible practices we see, without attending to the role these practices have in the overall lesson, novices are likely to use their newly acquired practices at the wrong times, in the wrong places, or for the wrong reasons'.

Kennedy's conclusion is that teacher education programmes often ignore the reasons for possessing the knowledge or applying the skills – the purpose of teaching is absent – and she offers an alternative conceptualisation of teaching practice as 'persistent problems' which are faced by all teachers, for which teachers must find workable solutions. She states that 'the role of teacher education is not to offer solutions to these problems, but instead to help novices learn to analyse these problems and to evaluate alternative courses of action for how well they address these problems'. The behaviours, knowledge and practices of teachers described in past attempts to parse the practice of teaching are not irrelevant in this model of teacher education, but instead form a body of knowledge which can be drawn upon to help teachers 'think strategically about how their actions address a larger purpose'.

Kennedy identifies a 'handful of important, meaningful, and analytically distinct purposes that teachers' actions serve', which she sets out as the 'persistent problems' faced by teachers:

- **Portraying the curriculum** content 'in a way that makes it comprehensible to naïve minds, and to decide how that portrait will be constructed from some kind of live activity that takes place in a specific space, uses specific materials, and occurs within a specific time frame';

- **Enlisting student participation** as 'education is mandatory but learning is not', therefore teachers face a captive, but sometimes resistant, audience;

- **Exposing student thinking** to ascertain what students 'understand, don't understand, or misunderstand', so that teachers know 'whether to repeat, elaborate or move on';

- **Containing student behaviour** so that students' attention is on the learning;

- **Accommodating personal needs** as teachers must find a way to perform their role in keeping with their personality and preferences, ensuring their job satisfaction and retention in the profession.

Parsing the practice of leadership

Kennedy's arguments are interesting and offer an alternative approach to solving the problem of parsing the practice of teaching. What might this perspective offer us in helping design a curriculum for the development of school leaders?

The history of leadership development programmes in England has many parallels to the evolution of teacher education curricula. School leadership has been parsed according to the knowledge required (often a

215

feature of university programmes), the specific actions leaders take and broader leadership behaviours (like the competency frameworks offered by national school leadership development programmes such as NCSL). The problems of grain size, loss of meaning and fads can be applied as readily to leadership development as to teacher education.

It may also be argued that the practice of teaching has many similarities to the practice of school leadership, and this suggests that Kennedy's proposed approach may be transferable to the problem of parsing the practice of leadership for the purpose of developing a curriculum and pedagogy. These similarities include:

- **Context:** Both take place within schools and present the practitioner with complex problems which can be solved in multiple ways. Neither teaching or school leadership offer clear pathways through these problems and there are uncertain relationships between action and consequence.

- **Human improvement:** Both may be considered to belong to a class of 'human improvement' professions[7] whereby one is reliant on the willingness of others (students/staff) to improve themselves.

- **Values:** Both teaching and leadership practice is driven by a moral purpose and practitioners are particularly value-driven. This feature means that both roles require much more than technical proficiency in a task; it is not only whether a goal is achieved, but whether the goal is the right one, that matters.

- **Fluid practice:** Expertise in both fields is characterised by what appears to be a seamless flow of application of tacit knowledge and skills, applied flexibly and responsively to emerging situations. Mechanistic responses ('when X happens, do Y') are rarely useful, as no two situations are the same.

Might it, therefore, be meaningful and possible to identify a similar set of 'persistent problems' around which a leadership curriculum could be based? What might these look like?

Kennedy offers various criteria throughout her paper against which we might judge any attempt to define a persistent problems framework.

Applied to leadership, these are as follows:

1. There should be only a 'handful of important, meaningful, and analytically distinct purposes' that leaders' actions serve;

2. Most observed leadership behaviours should be understandable in terms of how they help address one or more of these persistent problems;

3. The persistent problems identified must be unavoidable by school leaders as they perform their duties;

4. The problems will compete with each other 'in such a way that the solutions to one may interfere with success in another';

5. The challenges are universal across all contexts.

Let's give it a go. A literal translation of Kennedy's persistent problems may look like this:

The persistent problems teachers face	The persistent problems school leaders face
Portraying the curriculum	Portraying purpose and values
Enlisting student participation	Enlisting staff efforts
Exposing student thinking	Exposing indicators of change
Containing student behaviour	Resolving conflicts
Accommodating personal needs	Accommodating personal needs

Figure 1: Translating Kennedy's persistent problems faced by teachers into a school leadership context

Portraying purpose and values

No matter the context or specific role, school leaders are constantly challenged to define both the ultimate destination and short-term goals, and to portray this in such a way that others understand how things could be better than the current state of affairs.

Enlisting staff efforts

There is a reason why influence is often cited as a key characteristic of leadership behaviour. If individuals pursued their own goals, at their own pace, the school would be a chaotic place. School leaders must find ways of channelling attention and effort towards useful activity.

Exposing indicators of change

Leaders must be able to ascertain whether the school is changing in the desired ways, and if it isn't, why? School leaders must be responsive to these indicators, adjusting their strategies accordingly to achieve the stated goals. This concept is often narrowly defined as 'accountability' within today's schools, as leaders are expected to 'monitor standards' and 'intervene' where these are not high enough. However, such conceptualisations are a modern phenomenon and accountability has become a loaded term. The enduring moral duty of school leaders to discharge their responsibility to society by educating children well, and using the resources provided to them for this purpose equitably and efficiently, informs a broader motivation for understanding, whether the pace and direction of change is sufficient.

Resolving conflicts

School leadership inherently involves trade-offs, opportunity costs and dilemmas in decision-making. School leaders must find ways to reconcile competing priorities and find compromise. These conflicts may involve resource allocation decisions, value judgements about the curriculum, divided loyalties, power relations between staff, ethical decisions or fallout from catastrophic events. Resolving conflict is a daily feature of school leaders' roles, whatever their seniority.

Accommodating personal needs

Personality is a key determinant in leadership effectiveness, and while we can improve a leader's knowledge and skills, it is difficult to change who they are. Leaders operate stylistically in line with their values, beliefs and personality. Requiring them to adopt a style they feel uncomfortable with will inevitably lead to burnout. School leaders' personal needs around finding an acceptable balance between work and other aspects of life and being able to cope with the psychological demands of the job must also be accommodated. We have ignored this persistent problem of school leadership at our peril in recent years, making it increasingly difficult to recruit and retain leaders; particularly in senior positions.

The five persistent problems described provide a definition of what school leaders do:

- They portray a sense of purpose, and the core values which should underpin actions, through their daily interactions
- To influence others to expend their efforts towards achieving school effectiveness
- Which is made visible to decision makers so that strategies can be adjusted
- And conflicts can be resolved satisfactorily
- In a way that meets the leader's personal needs.

To what extent do these persistent problems of school leadership pass Kennedy's tests? There are a limited number of problems suggested, each of which appear to be important, meaningful, and analytically distinct. It is also difficult to imagine a leadership position in a school which would not meet these problems. A more junior role, such as the head of a subject department, would need to articulate direction and the principles which underpin their vision for the department, influence those in their team, check on progress on the journey to improvement, make numerous difficult decisions along the way and stay sane in the process! Equally, while on a grander scale, a headteacher would set out their vision and model the school's values through their everyday behaviour, create a culture which values staff efforts, ensure that senior leaders know the school well and are aware what progress is being made towards the school's goals, make fiendishly difficult decisions which may, at times, leave some parties dispossessed or disadvantaged, and avoid burnout along the way.

Anyone with experience of school leadership will quite easily imagine scenarios whereby the solutions to one of the above problems will impact upon the likely success of another. For example, the monitoring of standards necessary to know that they are improving can have adverse effects on staff morale; the need for leadership knowledge being traded off against the perception by the employee that they are trusted by leaders. In the current resource-restricted circumstance in UK schools, there are also clear trade-offs between controlling costs within funding limits and the achievement of organisational goals, building of capacity and the wellbeing of staff and leaders. Examples abound, so we can be confident that the persistent problems described meet Kennedy's requirement for competing purposes. It would appear that a fairly faithful translation of the persistent problems facing teachers to those school leaders grapple with gives us a reasonable first attempt at parsing leadership in this way.

A 'persistent problems' curriculum and pedagogy

What I like about Kennedy's approach to the parsing problem is that both the domain-specific knowledge and the application of this knowledge are valued, but only if these are explicitly connected to the purpose of solving the complex problems that leaders face in schools. This resonates with what we know about leadership expertise, which is that:

- Expert leaders have a vast schema of domain-specific knowledge; both technical knowledge and a deep understanding of the socio-cultural context within which they work;
- Expert leaders have learnt to apply their knowledge within different contexts and scenarios so that the knowledge becomes flexible, and their practice becomes fluid as the leader is able to quickly recognise underlying similarities in the structures of problems which point towards how to proceed;
- Expert leaders develop instinctive approaches to complex problems and are able to evaluate a range of alternative solutions, selecting a strategy which is deemed most likely to succeed.

A curriculum for school leadership will need to include both domain-specific content and the skills, techniques and approaches which leaders might employ. However, these might, productively, be explicitly connected through the curriculum and/or pedagogic approach to the persistent problems faced by school leaders.

For novice leaders, more explicit teaching of the curriculum content will be required as they will hold naive views of the complexity of the task of school leaders. Development programmes will need to equip participants with the domain-specific knowledge required, where this is not already possessed, and model how expert leaders draw on this knowledge to construct solutions to the problems they face. This may be achieved through case study material or, better, input from practising school leaders. The reasoning which leaders go through must be laid bare for novice leaders so that they begin to see the strategic thinking behind the decisions experts make. Participants in leadership programmes will also need opportunities to consider the problems faced in their own roles and context, learning to appreciate the importance of context in finding solutions and that solutions cannot be 'imported' from other schools. Ideally, there should be time and space in leadership programmes for participants to apply their learning in their school context and for structured reflection on this process. Such an approach will provide opportunities for novice leaders to consider their knowledge gaps in relation to specific problems, to work through their reasoning behind the decisions they make, to reflect on how skilfully they execute discrete components of the solution and retrospectively evaluate the process.

A 'persistent problems' framework provides a structure for thinking through the trade-offs made by leaders as they carry out their leadership role. By considering the competing purposes of the leadership endeavour, school leaders will come to understand the complexity of leadership and learn that multiple solutions exist to problems; none of which are perfect or without cost. This understanding will equip school leaders to deal with imperfection, uncertainty and even failure, which are all features of leadership in schools. This, in turn, will make them more resilient and likely to accommodate their own needs, and to not make excessive personal sacrifices in the pursuit of unattainable goals.

As leaders gain expertise, leadership programmes might focus less on domain-specific knowledge and more on the nuances of specific problems and contexts to provide leaders with the opportunity to fine-tune their understanding of complexity. Expert leaders will become more instinctive in their decision-making as their knowledge becomes tacit, but this risks leaders' assumptions being unexamined, therefore there should be opportunities to make reasoning explicit. Leadership programmes might, as a result, draw less on case studies and visiting experts, and more on the experiences of the participants on the programme: the curriculum therefore being co-constructed by the participants.

The limits of leadership education

There are many things we cannot hope to change through a leadership development programme. The leader's personality, their value system, mental acuity, memory strength and social attitudes will all be fairly fixed; at least in the short term (see Chapter 3). We are therefore unlikely to significantly alter the leader's motivations, their 'style' of leadership or their ability to process new information, and therefore how they respond in unfamiliar situations.

However, we can hope to equip leaders (within the usual time frames of a development programme) with new knowledge, perspectives and habits of mind. This offers hope that leadership education, if designed well, can impact on leadership effectiveness and make a tangible difference to how leaders perform their roles.

In my experience, there are three key reasons that leaders prove ineffective:

1. They do not possess the knowledge required to achieve their goals and fail to recognise this, and therefore to do something about it, before taking action. This knowledge might be technical or contextual; and/or,

2. They fail to think through the problem and possible solutions, applying reason to the task and considering fully the ramifications of different courses of action; and/or,

3. They select the wrong goals due to naivety or distraction.

I believe that there are two powerful things leaders can do to avoid these mistakes. Firstly, leaders should talk to staff about the school's problems and potential solutions as much as possible. Much of the knowledge they need is possessed by other adults within the school. Leaders need to have the humility to recognise that expert perspectives are held across the organisation. By tapping into this expert knowledge, leaders are less likely to select inadvisable goals and sub-optimal solutions.

Secondly, leaders should take the time to think about the problems faced and possible solutions carefully. Many bad decisions are made in haste.

Fortunately, leaders can get better at both of these powerful actions – namely information gathering and reasoning. And both can be developed through leadership programmes. If leadership education can help participants understand the importance of domain-specific knowledge and where this resides, and instil the habits of mind to slow down and think through problems and solutions carefully, they might make a permanent impact on leadership effectiveness, thereby leading to sustained improvements in our schools. This is a huge ambition for leadership development across the education system, but we should aim for no less. Leaders need help in finding sustainable solutions to the persistent problems they face.

Summary of chapter substance

■■■■■■■■ Substance (stuff) What do we need to know?	Leadership programmes must develop leaders' domain-specific knowledge, skills, techniques and core practices to equip them to solve the persistent problems they face. The curriculum and pedagogy for leadership education must be solutions-focused and equip leaders with the knowledge and habits of mind required to lead within the complex and nuanced contexts within which they work.
■■■■■■■■ Substance (significance) Why is this important?	Significant resources are employed in developing school leaders, and we know that leadership is one of the most important factors in school improvement. Leadership education programmes must have a tangible impact on the effectiveness of school leaders.
■■■■■■■■ Substance (validity) How do we know it to be true?	We know that expert leaders possess knowledge and skills, but moreover must draw on these to find solutions to meaningful problems. The *'why'* of leadership must come before the *'how'*, else we end up skilfully pursuing the wrong goals.

Further reading

I have drawn significantly from Mary Kennedy's excellent paper in this chapter and I would strongly recommend reading this in full (reference below).

References

1. Kennedy, M. (2016) 'Parsing the Practice of Teaching', *Journal of Teacher Education* 67 (1) pp. 6-17.

2. Charters, W. W. and Waples, D. (1929) *Commonwealth Teacher Training Study.* Chicago, IL: University of Chicago Press.

3. Forzani, F. M. (2014) 'Understanding "Core Practices" and "Practice-based" Teacher Education: Learning from the Past', *Journal of Teacher Education* 65 (4) pp. 357-368.

4. Shulman, L. S. (1987) 'Knowledge and Teaching: Foundations of the New Reform', *Harvard Educational Review* 57 pp. 1-22.

5. Ball, D. K. and Forzani, F. M. (2009) 'The Work of Teaching and the Challenge for Teacher Education', *Journal of Teacher Education* 60 (5) pp. 497-511.

6. Grossman, P., Hammerness, K. and McDonald, M. (2009) 'Redefining Teaching, Re-imagining Teacher Education', *Teachers and Teaching: Theory and Practice* 15 (2) pp. 273-289.

7. Cohen, D. K. (2011) *Teaching and its Predicaments.* Cambridge, MA: Harvard University Press.

Chapter 18
Failure to learn

Leaders have a symbiotic relationship with the schools they lead. Where this relationship is positive, each will be nourished by the other. Nourishment for the leader comes in the form of feedback: information which they must be open to receiving and acting upon. Nourishment for the school comes in the form of the actions leaders take to enrich the organisation. School improvement depends on this symbiosis, and where it breaks down, each party becomes poisonous to the other.

A symbiotic leadership perspective is consistent with the view of leadership espoused in these pages. Rather than considering leaders as God-like figures upon whose omnipotence school success depends, we should see them as part of the ecosystem. Leaders should acquire a detailed knowledge of the school in which they lead and build contextualised expertise by positioning themselves to receive information, or intelligence, so that they may make sense of complexity and make decisions which gradually and subtly steering the school to success.

The nature and accuracy of the information a leader receives, the way the leader perceives the information, and how they respond, are critical factors in the symbiotic cycle. Where leadership genericism is dominant, we have seen how decisions can be affected by poorly selected measures of success; whether it be league table positions, flight paths or graded lesson observations. I have argued that a leader's decision-making can be affected by an overly empathic response, grand visions, self-importance, whimsical theories of leadership, or a willingness to set aside one's values in pursuit of self-interest or the 'quick win'. Conversely, I have argued that leaders who carefully consider the indicators of success, actively seek out feedback and interpret this information rationally and knowledgeably, will make better decisions. The tendency and ability to make rational sense of organisational complexity lies at the heart of expert leadership. Even when things are going well, it is difficult to be the type of leader advocated; in the face of difficulty, it becomes even harder. Failure, or the threat of failure, can be toxic to a healthy symbiotic relationship.

How schools respond to failure is fundamentally important. Failure is potentially corrosive, as it is bound up (at least, in most cultures) with feelings of shame, embarrassment or fear by those who have failed, and as a signal of incompetence or negligence by those who look on. As a result, failure is often hidden; particularly from those in authority. This is highly problematic for leaders, resulting in a false view of the success of school policy or a delayed response to matters which may escalate if left unaddressed. The more personal the failure, the greater the attempt to hide it. In schools, it is often the failure that happens inside the teacher's classroom which leaders are least likely to hear about: the class whose behaviour is deteriorating or who are making little progress in their learning. Where such failure goes undiscovered for some time before coming to the attention of school leaders, the response may be to implement systems which attempt to identify problems earlier: more frequent data collection, observation of lessons, work scrutiny. Leaders signal that teachers cannot be left alone to do their jobs without supervision, but in doing so, reinforce the desire to hide failure, as the teacher expects to be met with blame rather than support. The poison introduced into the symbiotic relationship between leaders and the school is mistrust, which leads to a further breakdown in the information flow to leaders. As leaders know less and less about what is really going on, they depend more and more on audit evidence, which is fabricated to present a rosy image of the school. Overcoming the human tendency to hide failure is critical to creating an organisational culture in which leaders have accurate information on which to assess improvement efforts and decide where their attention should best be directed.

Open loop systems

In Matthew Syed's book, *Black Box Thinking*,[1] the author describes organisational cultures in which failure leads to progress rather than decline. Syed examines the culture which has developed in aviation whereby failure (in the form of accidents and near misses) are systematically and openly picked apart and the lessons learnt are used to inform improvements in safety. Over time, this has resulted in an incredible safety record for the commercial airline industry. Syed calls this approach an 'open loop system', meaning that failure leads to progress, as feedback is rationally acted upon. This, he argues, is radically different to the 'closed loop system' found in healthcare, whereby mistakes are hidden, go unrecorded and subsequently do not lead to improvement.

Fundamental to an open loop system is the willingness of individuals to admit their mistakes. This requires people to feel 'safe' in drawing attention to failure, knowing that the outcome will be better for them if they do so. Safety means that no blame will be attached (protecting a sense of self-worth) and people will come and help out (making the individual's work easier). There might also be a sense that, by admitting that something is wrong, you may help prevent future problems and be a part of the success of the whole system. It must be made psychologically attractive to admit failure for an open loop system to take hold. Syed illustrates the desired culture through the example of a system adopted by Toyota in their manufacturing plants, whereby workers would pull a cord when something went wrong. The result was that a cluster of senior managers would almost immediately appear to help resolve the problem. This system only worked once the workers trusted that the mistake could be openly admitted and the senior managers were focused on finding a solution, not looking to blame.

The Toyota example illustrates the idea of a 'team around the problem' (TAP). A TAP approach requires that people with the right expertise are called on to solve the 'swampy' problems often arising in school contexts. Such an approach can often be seen in schools in relation to blameless problems – for example, finding a way to support a child with difficult home circumstances – but not in relation to failure of the school or its employees. Could we envisage a culture whereby teachers could immediately call in support to help get a lesson back on track without fear of blame or a label of weakness, or admitting that they cannot 'control the class'? If teachers felt able to 'pull the cord' and bring the right expertise to bear on the problems they faced, how much healthier would the school be as a result?

Error signals

Just as teachers need feedback from students to check that what they have taught has been understood, leaders need feedback on their impact, too. To illustrate the importance of feedback, Syed uses a golfing analogy, whereby a golfer looks at the accuracy of each ball played and uses this feedback to subtly adjust his swing, gradually becoming a better player over time. Without the benefit of feedback, Syed argues, we are like golfers playing in the dark. Particularly important are 'error signals': indicators that things are going wrong. Where there is a fear of failure, leaders do not receive as many error signals and can be lulled into a false sense of security.

Many error signals in schools come from complaints (by students, staff or parents), therefore it is easy for leaders to become defensive and seek to justify their actions rather than treat the complaint as a useful piece of feedback. I was cornered by a parent at a parents' evening recently who wanted to complain about the information sent out by the school: the frequency, content, format and so forth. We had made considerable improvements to our communications with parents over the previous couple of years, introducing a weekly bulletin, revamping the website and initiating quality control on all letters, therefore my emotional reaction was to bristle at the criticism. I wanted to explain how much better our communications were compared to before, but this was obviously irrelevant to the parent; their perception was to do with how effective our communications were against their expectations, not against past standards. The parent talked me through their concerns and finished by apologising for moaning. They were surprised when I thanked them for giving me some really useful feedback. The reason it is so difficult to respond in this way is twofold: firstly, we take the criticism personally, particularly if we have invested in improving this aspect of the school; secondly, most people are really bad at providing constructive criticism, tending to talk in terms of what is negative rather than how things could be even better. As leaders, we need to listen to the substance of the feedback, not the style in which it is delivered. Complaints are valuable error signals, but if we respond emotionally to these, then this valuable source of information will dry up.

Interpreting feedback

As well as creating a culture in which individuals are willing to admit mistakes and leaders welcome error signals as useful feedback, Syed lastly makes a case for caution in interpreting the data we have access to. He cites the work of Abraham Wald during the Second World War. Wald became involved in trying to improve survival rates for fighter pilots. To do this, the returning planes were examined to establish where the bullets had hit and, therefore, where additional armour was needed. This data showed that the tail and cockpit were rarely hit and therefore no more armour was required in these areas. Wald pointed out that the data was flawed. The useful data was on the planes which had not returned. Wald inferred that the absence of bullet holes on the tail and cockpit were the reason for these planes returning, and that those which had been brought down had been hit in these areas. The conclusion was that the additional armour should, in fact, be placed exactly where the bullet holes did not appear. This counterintuitive reasoning drastically improved the survival rates of British pilots.

As leaders, we should take account of all the available data, but also that which is not immediately available. We must be careful to avoid interpreting data in a way that confirms our existing beliefs. For example, we often look at the traits of students who are successful at school and draw conclusions about the reasons for their success. We may notice that they work hard and infer that this is a key reason for their academic achievement, which it may well be, but what about all those students who worked hard and didn't do as well? By examining the circumstances around those who have the 'desirable' traits but do not achieve success, we may learn more about how to enable students to achieve well in the future. School leaders may learn more about where the additional armour is required by paying attention to the planes that don't come back: the examples of failure rather than the obvious successes.

Trial and error

The nature of schools is such that we often don't know whether something will work until it has been put into practice; there are invariably unintended consequences and butterfly effects. For this reason, sensitivity to error signals is particularly important. Due to the unforeseeable outcomes of school improvement efforts, radical change is particularly risky, as changing many factors at once will have the potential to tip the unpredictable into the chaotic. In his book, *Adapt*,[2] the economist Tim Harford makes a powerful case against top-down design in complex systems such as schools, arguing instead for a more evolutionary trial and error approach. Harford gives the example of the development of a particular nozzle needed in the production of washing powder. Unilever had employed their best mathematicians to design a nozzle that would create the fine powder required. Their designs failed. In desperation, they turned to a team of biologists. They had no idea how to design a solution to the problem, but they did have an approach for finding one. The team took ten random designs and tested them. The most effective nozzle was selected and ten slightly varied versions produced. The process was repeated, and after 45 generations and 449 failures, the final highly effective nozzle was produced.

Harford uses the term 'God complex' to refer to our tendency to believe we know how the world works, when often we don't. These ideas resonate strongly with me. I believe that school leaders are frequently guilty of possessing a God complex and attempting to design and impose systems and policies in a complex context with no evidence that these will be effective. Senior leaders are full of 'good ideas' but their whimsical policy making can be damaging and undermine confidence. It is possible to run schools in a different way. Let's take the example of a school's behaviour management approach. These are, in my experience, designed and redesigned with little evidence of what works. Why? It is surely possible to evolve a more effective system through careful trial and error. This would need to be a disciplined approach with clear criteria set for evaluating success. To be completely sure, a Randomised Controlled Trial (RCT) could be set up with a control group as a point of comparison. Alternatively, Unilever's approach of trying out various methods and evolving variants on the most effective iteration could be employed. Most of the methods tried would fail, or at least not be as successful as they could be, but the end result would be an approach which has evolved through adaptation and selection. As with the origins of humankind, evolution trumps intelligent design.

A trial and error approach to managing change in schools casts the school leader as TV weatherman Phil Connors in the 1993 movie, *Groundhog Day*. In the film, Connors, played brilliantly by Bill Murray, is caught in a time loop and made to live the same day again and again. Connors uses this freedom to try living the day in a multitude of different ways, each time finding out the consequences of his actions. He tries in vain to win the affection of his colleague, Rita; each day subtly changing his approach, having learnt from his past failings. Finally, Connors succeeds in breaking the cycle when he professes to Rita that he has fallen in love with her, completing his transition from an embittered weatherman to a vulnerable and genuine person. While the daily experiences of school leaders may not be as romantic or narratively satisfying as *Groundhog Day*, the idea that every day is a new opportunity to fail in a different way, to gradually move towards success, is appealing. Trial and error, on this scale is low risk and makes a virtue of failure; it is the antithesis of the high-stakes, failure-averse culture that exists in many schools.

Learning through experience

A healthy, symbiotic relationship between leader and school provides the most fertile ground for leadership development as well as school development. Open loop systems help leaders overcome the Dunning-Kruger effect (discussed in Chapter 17), particularly where leaders are exposed and responsive to error signals. Failure is not only inevitable in schools: it is crucial in securing improvement. The attitude that school leaders have towards failure will be significant in creating a growth culture, and leaders will be the beneficiaries of this culture as they receive better feedback on their decisions and impact. Failure is integral to learning and should be cherished by leaders.

Summary of chapter substance

▬▬▬▬▬▬▬▬ **Substance (stuff)** What do we need to know?	Failure provides an excellent opportunity for schools to learn and develop. School leaders should create a culture in which individuals feel safe in drawing attention to failure. Harnessing expertise to work out what went wrong builds organisational resilience and future success.
▬▬▬▬▬▬▬ **Substance (significance)** Why is this important?	If leaders respond in the wrong way to mistakes, mistrust develops and failure will be hidden rather than learnt from. In such cultures, both leadership development and school improvement will be hindered.
▬▬▬▬▬▬ **Substance (validity)** How do we know it to be true?	Lessons can be learnt from industries and organisations which have embedded open loop systems; for example in aviation, where there have been significant improvements in safety as a result of a culture which seeks to learn from mistakes.

References

1. Syed, M. (2015), *Black Box Thinking*. London: John Murray Publishers.

2. Harford, T. (2012), *Adapt: Why Success Always Starts with Failure*. London: Little, Brown.

Chapter 19
Leadership knowledge

In my experience, upon finding oneself in a leadership position, the training and support we need is rarely forthcoming. We are often left to find our own way, expected to use the 'skills' we have to work it out. If we are lucky, someone in a more senior position may take us under their wing, or we may be given a mentor. We might be told we should join a leadership programme, but these will often teach abstract notions of leadership and fail to address the substance of the task at hand. More often than not, we will develop through exposure to the multitude of 'swampy problems' we encounter; sometimes getting lucky, but mostly making mistakes and vowing to make better decisions next time.

When left to our own devices, how should we proceed? Our goal is fluid expertise;[1] the ability to solve the tricky problems we are likely to encounter in our context deftly and appropriately. Our starting point is as a novice; not only do we lack the knowledge we will need, but we are also blissfully ignorant of our ignorance. The entry point for leaders is not to set about understanding leadership directly, but to acquire a base of knowledge across other domains.

Everything but leadership

Perhaps the biggest mistake we make as leaders is to assume that we need to know more about leadership. The curriculum for leadership programmes is filled with theory from this ill-defined domain and leadership literature presents off-the-shelf models which we are encouraged to apply to our varying contexts. However, the best leaders I have known do not spend their time studying leadership. There are far more reputable disciplines from which we can draw our expertise, such as economics, philosophy, political science, history and social psychology.[2] There is plenty of theory and evidence relevant to the task of leadership, but relatively little of it comes from the disciplinary field of leadership.

In the discipline of economics, an understanding of opportunity cost will help leaders consider policy not only from the perspective of the benefits an initiative will bring, but with regard to the foregone benefits of the alternative ways time, energy and resource might have been deployed (perhaps the recent obsession with dialectic marking would have been arrested earlier if leaders factored opportunity cost into their decision-making?). Economic game theory provides insight for leaders into how decision-making is affected by an expectation of how others will behave and respond. Given that our national examination system is based on a zero-sum game, whereby the gains of one agent will lead to an equal loss of another, school leaders operate in game-playing scenarios where school improvement requires strategic understanding. Economists also provide insights into how we respond to incentives. The infant field of 'nudge' economics, a branch of behavioural economics, helps leaders gently shift behaviour towards desirable ends.[3] For example, nudge economics has recently been applied to the task of improving school attendance by demonstrating that rewards for 100% attendance might be counter-productive, as they send a signal that attending school every day is exceptional and only expected of a minority.[4]

Behavioural economics moves us towards the field of psychology, which also has much to offer in our quest for leadership knowledge. Psychology helps us understand human motivation and relations, without both of which no leader can hope to be successful. School leaders must learn how to harness intrinsic motivation, create an environment which promotes wellbeing, and influence others without coercion. How often have we seen leaders ignorant of the basics of psychology doing untold damage to the schools they lead? Also, the emerging field of cognitive science increasingly provides insight for school leaders about how we learn, and this understanding is having a significant impact on how we provide education across many schools.

School leaders should also acquire a philosophical perspective. Philosophy tempers an overly instrumentalist view of leadership, leading us to question the moral purpose of our actions. Many of the problems faced by leaders are ethical dilemmas, or at least have an ethical dimension. Philosophy also protects against narrow educational purposes, reminding us that there are different ways of knowing and being. Philosophy teaches us about truth, believed by some to be the ultimate purpose of education. It also teaches us to be sceptical, questioning, considered.

We must draw knowledge from across these disciplines and more: an understanding of social justice and inequality acquired through the study of sociology; a grasp of statistical validity from mathematics; an insight into the use and misuse of power from the field of political science. Rather than turn to the leadership canon, we should look first to the wealth of human disciplinary knowledge. School leaders can do no better than to be the model of an educated person, broad in their knowledge and inquisitive by nature. Is that not what we expect our students to be?

Tiers of leadership knowledge

The inter-disciplinary knowledge described above is not related specifically to schools, at least until it is applied to educational problems. For the purposes of this chapter, I will call this 'Tier 1' leadership knowledge; that is knowledge drawn from a variety of disciplines which has a bearing on the typical challenges faced by school leaders. Tier 1 knowledge ensures that the leader is 'educated' in the broadest sense, but leaves us far short of the expert knowledge we need; it is necessary but not sufficient.

Leaders will also require knowledge which relates directly to the problems encountered in schools in particular. This 'Tier 2' domain will include technical knowledge about the economic, social, political and legislative context within which schools operate. Technical knowledge can be acquired generally, but it is impossible for a leader to acquire and retain all the technical knowledge they will need to solve the range of problems they encounter. Technical knowledge will therefore often be acquired on a need-to-know basis. In education, technical knowledge may include areas of employment law, equality, special educational needs, medical conditions, government policy, technology, the National Curriculum and assessment framework, or finance. Tier 2 knowledge, like Tier 1, is independent of school context.

Next, the leader needs a detailed knowledge of the organisation in which they lead: contextual knowledge which includes an understanding of the social and cultural aspects of the school. This 'Tier 3' knowledge is specific to the school, but until it is pulled into a decision-making process, it remains a broad, general knowledge base. Tier 3 knowledge includes what the leader knows about the personal and professional characteristics of employees, how individuals and teams relate to each other, norms of behaviour and the expectations members of the organisation hold about how events will progress into the future. Unlike Tier 1 and 2 knowledge, which can be carried between contexts, Tier 3 knowledge is 'situated' i.e. specific to the context. Combining Tier 1, 2 and 3 knowledge helps leaders form hypotheses about how an event may play out. For example, leaders might generally expect some resistance if they increase the level of scrutiny of curriculum decisions made by subject leaders, whatever school they are in. However, knowledge of the particular context will help the leader form a theory on how significant this resistance will be. If subject leaders have historically had significant autonomy over most aspects of their work, then it is likely that they will resist leaders' interference more robustly. Conversely, if their experience has been that working closely with senior leaders has resulted in improvements in other aspects, such as teaching standards, we might expect greater co-operation.

Tiers 1 to 3 get progressively more specific. Tier 1 knowledge is broad, general knowledge, drawn from a range of disciplines, relevant to the moral and practical challenges of leadership. Tier 2 knowledge is pertinent to the school system in particular. Tier 3 knowledge is specific to the school in which we lead. The possession of these tiers of knowledge is a pre-requisite to developing expertise, but does not constitute expertise in itself. Tier 1 to 3 knowledge can be acquired through 'study', either in the academic sense or by being observant of our surroundings, but expertise moves us from knowing something to being able to solve problems with that knowledge.

How novice leaders solve problems

The challenge for novice leaders is to turn their explicit, inflexible knowledge into tacit, flexible knowledge which enables them to solve a wide range of ill-defined, messy problems. This is only possible through repeated practice.

When novices encounter problems, they have limited experience of similar problems to inform their decisions. Therefore, the knowledge they bring to bear is drawn from Tiers 1 to 3, acquired through study rather than experience. Novices may be able to speculate as to how a scenario will play out but their hypothesis will be purely theoretical and pieced together through a conscious analysis of the situation. They will have few 'rules of thumb' (heuristics) to shortcut their thinking, therefore each stage and aspect of the problem must be taken in turn for consideration. Novices can become bogged down in the detail or overloaded with information; they may lose sight of the big picture, as their working memory is absorbed with each element of the complex scenario and its possible solutions. It is tempting for novice leaders to rely heavily on published procedure and 'do it by the book', as established rules provide a hand-hold for working through the problem. Time may be spent looking up the technical knowledge required, or consulting those with the expertise in the relevant area.

Leading as a novice is hard work. Progress is slow and frustrating, and leaders will encounter frequent setbacks and make lots of mistakes. However, each experience will provide the leader with tacit knowledge which will be stored as a reference point for when similar problems are encountered later. Initially, specific lessons will be learnt which relate to the particular problem encountered, but over time, the leader will learn to recognise the similarities in structures of similar problems and develop mental models of the various 'problem states' they typically encounter. These models will help the leader identify shortcuts in their thinking, which will speed up decision-making and enable leaders to focus their attention on what makes this problem subtly different from the others experienced. These mental models are Tier 4 knowledge: tacit, internalised understanding which enables the leader to think intuitively and become procedurally fluent. Tier 4 knowledge is flexible and transferable; it incorporates the general Tier 1 to 3 knowledge relevant to the specific problem, thereby making this knowledge domain-specific and integral to the mental model in this particular scenario.

Possession of Tier 4 knowledge allows the expert to mentally take a step back; to commit intellectual resources to overseeing the problem-solving approach[3]. This meta-cognition, or strategic thinking ability, means expert leaders maintain a big picture view; for example, assessing whether the decisions made are consistent with the values and goals of the leader and/or organisation. This 'Tier 5' knowledge is the hallmark of the true expert.

The fundamentally different ways that experts and novices employ their mental resources when solving complex problems means that novices cannot shortcut to expertise by mimicking how experts solve problems. Experts have the 'curse of knowledge' as they will find it hard to imagine what it was like to lack expertise. Novices can, therefore, be helped to learn their craft, but the instruction or advice of experts is unlikely to be helpful. Novices must develop expertise through a process of experimentation, feedback and reflection.

It takes time to develop leadership expertise. A leader's knowledge must be broad and extensive, but expertise means anchoring this knowledge to specific problems, making it tacit and flexible. Little of the knowledge leaders need will come from the field of leadership. Leaders must instead acquire technical and disciplinary knowledge, study the schools in which they lead and, finally, master the specific problems they encounter, if they are to learn the art of leadership.

Summary of chapter substance

▬▬▬▬▬ **Substance (stuff)** What do we need to know?	Becoming an expert leader takes time. Leaders must possess a vast repertoire of declarative knowledge across many disciplinary fields, technical knowledge relating to the domain of education, and an understanding of the social and cultural context within which they lead. However, this knowledge does not constitute expertise, which is characterised by the tacit, problem-specific knowledge which leaders develop through repeated exposure to complex and ambiguous problems. Expert knowledge is flexible and fluid, and cannot be learnt by study or observation.

▓▓▓▓▓▓▓▓ **Substance (significance)** Why is this important?	School leaders will only learn expertise through trial and error. An understanding of how expertise is developed will help leaders deal with the setbacks and be patient in their quest to become a better leader.
▓▓▓▓▓▓▓▓ **Substance (validity)** How do we know it to be true?	Expertise research is wide ranging and produces reasonably consistent results about the process of moving from being a novice to an expert. This field is supported by an emerging understanding from cognitive science about how knowledge is acquired and applied.

Further reading

Although there are many books about education and leadership referenced throughout this text, my knowledge of leading schools has been influenced by a much wider range of literature. I would like to reference some of these here, with a brief explanation about how I have found them relevant to my understanding of education.

Economics

The field of economics has a great deal to offer in helping understand the behaviour of humans and social groups.

Syed, M. (2015) *Black Box Thinking*. London: John Murray Publishers.
A book about failure and how to create a culture that utilises it for good. Schools are built on failure; harness it.

Taleb, N. N. (2012) *Antifragile: Things that Gain from Disorder*. London: Penguin.
How to deal with randomness and find strength in fragility. When the world is falling apart, leaders must find strength and ways to gain from chaos.

Cassidy, J. (2009) *How Markets Fail: The Logic of Economic Calamities*. London: Penguin.
Essential to understanding why we're in the state we're in.

Roberts, R. (2014) *How Adam Smith Can Change Your Life: An Unexpected Guide to Human Nature and Happiness*. London: Penguin Books.
A meditation on virtue and becoming a better person which is, after all, what education is all about.

Levitt, S. D. and Dubner, S. J. (2006) *Freakonomics*. London: Penguin.
Helps you think about everything in a different way.

Wilkinson, R. and Pickett, K. (2009) *The Spirit Level: Why Equality is Better for Everyone*. London: Penguin.
This book changed my view on poverty and inequality. If you want to understand advantage gaps in schools, you must read this.

Surowiecki, J. (2004) *The Wisdom of Crowds: Why the Many Are Smarter Than the Few*. New York, NY: Doubleday & Co.

This book helped me to understand that, on average, everyone else is probably right, and I am probably wrong. Listening to the voice of students, staff and parents brings great insight.

Psychology and the mind

The business of schools is learning, and to foster this, an understanding of the human mind is essential. This knowledge is equally important in leading people towards a shared goal of educational excellence.

Kahneman, D. (2011) *Thinking Fast and Slow*. New York, NY: Farrar, Straus and Giroux.
Exposes the bias in our thinking, to which every leader falls foul.

Lewis, M. (2017) *The Undoing Project*. London: Penguin.
The story of Daniel Kahneman and Amos Tversky, whose work changed our understanding of the human mind.

Cain, S. (2012) *Quiet: The Power of Introverts in a World That Can't Stop Talking*. London: Penguin.
You don't have to be loud and brash to be a leader; in fact, it is a disadvantage. Quiet leaders will one day rule the world.

Bloom, P. (2018) *Against Empathy: The Case for Rational Compassion*. London: Penguin.
Schools can seem full of bleeding hearts. It isn't helpful. Compassion is essential, but empathy is a dangerous distraction.

Gardner, D. (2008) *Risk: The Science and Politics of Fear*. London: Virgin Books.
How fear prevents us thinking rationally. There is so much fear in education and this distorts leaders' decisions and distracts them from a moral purpose.

Philosophy

Leadership is underpinned by beliefs and values. We, as leaders, need to know what we stand for and be able to justify our moral stance.

Gaarder, J. (1995) *Sophie's World*. New York, NY: Farrar, Straus and Giroux.
Leaders need to be philosophers. This is the most entertaining way to learn different ways to see the world.

Gray, J. (2002) *Straw Dogs; Thoughts on Humans and Other Animals*. London: Granta Publications.
What does it mean to be human in the early 21st century?

Haig, M. (2015) *Reasons to Stay Alive*. Edinburgh: Canongate Books.
Unless you have lived through severe mental health problems, you probably can't imagine what it may be like. And yet, adults and children in our schools suffer deeply. How can we begin to understand mental illness?

Pirsig, R. M. (1974) *Zen and the Art of Motorcycle Maintenance*. London: Vintage.
Awash in managerial conceptions of quality, it pays to consider what really gives something value.

Blackburn, S. (1999) *Think*. Oxford: Oxford University Press.

Thinking clearly and rationally is essential to leadership. How do we cut through the complexity?

Blackburn, S. (2005) *Truth: A Guide for the Perplexed*. London: Penguin.

Education may be defined as the pursuit of truth. Do we, as leaders, have a grasp of the purpose of education?

Science and mathematics

Science has transformed our society and is beginning to transform education. However, we must learn to handle evidence and be able to question its validity in an educational context.

Henderson, M. (2010) *The Geek Manifesto*. London: Bantam Press.

How can we harness scientific methodology to understand the mind, education and organisations?

Goldacre, B. (2008) *Bad Science*. London: Fourth Estate.

What can education learn from the use and misuse of science in other fields?

Goldacre, B. (2014) *I Think You'll Find It's a Bit More Complicated Than That*. London: Fourth Estate.

Many education policies are based on whim, ideology and 'good ideas'. How do we form evidence-based policy?

Ellenberg, J. (2014) *How Not to be Wrong: The Hidden Maths of Everyday Life*. London: Penguin.

Education is full of lies, damn lies and statistics. School leaders need a grasp of numbers to fight their corner.

References

1. For a clear and concise explanation of expertise see: Didau, D. (2019) *Making Kids Cleverer: A Manifesto for Closing the Advantage Gap*. Camarthen, Wales: Crown House Publishing Limited, pp. 233-241.

2. Washbush, J. B. (2005) 'There is no such thing as leadership', revisited, *Management Decisions* 43.

3. For examples of the application of nudge theory to the task of improving attendance in schools, see: Jordan, P. W. (2018) 'Nudging Students and Families to Better Attendance', EducationNext [Online], 11 May. Retrieved from: www.bit.ly/2K1kmFE

4. George, L. (2018) 'Why rewarding 100% attendance can be damaging', Tes [Online], 25 September. Retrieved from: www.bit.ly/2pKJwCm

Chapter 20
A new leadership orthodoxy

Despite the undoubted desire of most leaders to be as good as they can be, recent history demonstrates that school leaders are a product of the system within which they work. Leaders, like everyone, will do what is expected of them, and tend towards the norm. If genericism is the orthodoxy, it is either brave, or incredibly stupid, to resist its pull.

The very forces which have led us astray must be harnessed to encourage leaders to focus on the substance of education. Our school system needs a reboot: as does the way we think about school leadership.

Government policy

Politics frequently over-reaches itself when it comes to education policy. Education secretaries cannot resist tinkering: injecting 'ring-fenced' pots of money for schools to pursue particular projects and launching endless initiatives. Their actions are distractions for school leaders: bribes and coercion to pursue goals other than those pertinent to their own context. The pet projects of the education secretary often reflect a misunderstanding of the purposes of education and the way schools work. For example, as I write, Damian Hinds has launched the next phase of his 'character education' strategy, condemned by traditionalists and progressives alike as reflecting a complete misunderstanding of how young people develop as a result of their educational experience. This is what happens when non-experts make policy.

Of course, state schools are funded through taxation, therefore the government has a responsibility to ensure this money is spent well, and a right to set strategic priorities. Government has an important role to play in creating a framework within which schools operate. This framework might include teacher training, regulation, safeguarding and social policy. However, the substance of education should remain free of political interference: namely what schools teach, how they teach and how this is assessed and accredited. Schools need protection from the ideological whims of politicians on the left and right, and the policies designed to play well in *The Daily Mail* or *The Guardian*. That is not to say that there should be no centralised curriculum or assessment policy, rather that it should be set by a body independent of government. Just like when control of interest rates was handed over to the Bank of England by Gordon Brown in 1997, we need a government brave enough to accept that they are not best placed to be driving policy around the school curriculum.

Rather than interfere in school matters, the government might instead focus on the societal problems which make it more difficult for schools to achieve their goals. Schools have become the scapegoat for society's ills and the means of delivering the solutions. Schools are required to close disadvantage gaps, address mental health problems, repair the damage caused by social media, prevent domestic violence, spot potential terrorists, reduce obesity, and all manner of other things. Schools undoubtedly have a role to play in all of the above, but they cannot solve these problems alone. If government wants our schools to compete on a world stage with the likes of Singapore, it should make it as easy as possible for them to focus on the things that will improve students' knowledge. Raising attainment in literacy would be so much easier were it not for disadvantage gaps, but these gaps arise from the inequalities in society, not in our schools. The best education policy is policy which reduces the societal issues that distract schools from teaching the curriculum really well.

School accountability

Schools must be open to scrutiny. The dilemma facing any inspectorate is how to gain an insight into standards while limiting 'observer effects' (i.e. schools changing what they do as a result of being scrutinised), or at least ensuring that the changes in behaviour are beneficial to the children in our schools. Ofsted face a similar problem to school leaders in that it is incredibly difficult to assess standards in relation to many aspects of a school's work: learning cannot be seen; progress is not linear; lesson observations are not reliable in judging teacher effectiveness; and cause and effect relationships are unclear in relation to most educational purposes. Acknowledging the difficulty of reaching reliable judgements through a short inspection, Ofsted have come to rely instead on quality-assuring the headteacher's judgements about standards, which has had the consequence of creating audit trails throughout the school system and promoting a managerial culture (see Chapter 6).

Ofsted's 2019 Education Inspection Framework (EIF) signals a new focus on the 'substance' of education; it is less about exam results and progress data, and more about the curriculum and the entirety of the educational experience. The EIF might discourage leadership genericism through its focus on more meaningful aspects of a school's work, and in this regard it is welcome, but it will not lessen the tendency for school leaders to 'prove' that the school meets expectations. Even before the EIF came into force in September 2019, there were indications that schools were busy preparing documentation to evidence their thinking about the curriculum. The audit culture has a new focus.

The behaviour of school leaders faced with Ofsted is rational but not desirable. The stakes are so high that leaders will jump through whatever hoops they need to in order to avoid being downgraded by Ofsted. To break the cycle, at least two things need to change. Firstly, the grading system used by Ofsted should go. It is the label which instils the fear of Ofsted and causes parents to desert their local school, staff to leave and headteachers to be sacked. A qualitative report need be no less incisive or critical; indeed, we might focus on the content of the report all the more if the label were not distracting us. Secondly, Ofsted must recognise that some aspects of school standards should be scrutinised through methods other than inspection. Inspection works best for matters of compliance (e.g. finance, safeguarding, health and safety, exam practices) and aspects of school standards which are observable and measurable (e.g. attendance, behaviour, exclusions, adherence to the National Curriculum). It is not effective for reaching conclusions about the core business of schools (e.g. teaching, learning, student progress, wellbeing, personal development, ethos). To ensure standards in these areas, there needs to be someone independent of the school to make assessment of the quality of education over time. This may be achieved, for example, through an accredited and regulated body of school improvement partners who work closely with school leaders to improve educational outcomes. School standards can be assured through reliable, first-hand witness accounts rather than trails of paperwork and a high-stakes inspection. This will focus leaders not on the next inspection, but on sustained improvements in standards over time.

School structures

The legal status of our schools continues to be a pre-occupation of government and a potential distraction for school leaders. My concern is not whether multi-academy trusts (MATs) are better or worse than local authority-maintained schools or single academies, but whether they lead to further genericism, or instead enable leaders to focus on what is best for the students in their schools. The jury is out on this matter. The risk is that larger, corporate structures will demand uniformity and impose abstract performance measures on schools. The duty on the MAT is to improve the quality of education in its schools, and to do this it must 'know' what the current standards are. But this presents a similar problem to that faced by Ofsted, in that it is tempting to make these judgements using simplified metrics and burdensome evidence collection.

This imperative can override decisions which might actually lead to better educational outcomes. For example, there are MATs which have synchronised data collection methods and timings, such that the cycle of assessment across schools is dictated by the need for performance measures rather than the needs of the students and nature of the content being taught. However, MATs do not inevitably lead to more genericism. If leaders with substance are in charge, there are significant opportunities to tackle genericism. For example, curriculum expertise can be pooled to improve curriculum design and the quality of resources and assessment materials. MAT structures may also provide greater opportunities for peer networks and professional learning communities, displacing the need for excessive 'leadership' as expert practitioners work together to raise standards. As in any organisation, leaders will have a role to play in influencing the culture and systems; we need to ensure that MAT leaders understand the trappings of leadership genericism and the limitations of leadership.

Leadership development

While the things leaders do are important, we must stop glorifying leadership as a calling, and as a field of enquiry. Often, leadership is not what is required, and when it is, it is probably not the sort of leadership that typically comes to mind. Leadership development programmes reinforce a geocentric view of leadership by placing the leader as the central character in the school improvement story. Almost everything they teach is about leadership, when leading is only one fraction of what those in authority do. We need a new language to talk about leadership; one which reflects the gritty, contextualised, messy, ill-defined, ambiguous problems encountered by leaders; the imperfection of solutions and necessity of failure. The gaps in our expertise should not be highlighted by comparing ourselves to great leaders (or idealised leadership models), but by identifying that which we do not yet know enough about, or have sufficient experience in doing. Our future leaders must understand the dangers of genericism: belief in generic leadership skills, theories of everything, superficial goals, transient change, distraction, abstraction, grand visions and heroic endeavours, ideology, mythology, and style over substance.

What remains?

At the beginning of this book, I professed my scepticism, claiming that leadership may be neither a distinct nor useful concept. Having explored deeper into this jungle, I have found signs of a lost city: tantalising artefacts which draw me further still. It feels like there is something of substance hidden in the tangled vines and dense undergrowth: something buried and obfuscated. I am hopeful that we will find something, but it might not be the city of gold that we imagined. I would be happy with a modest settlement made of stone: evidence that someone once did something humble – of service to their community. In the end, perhaps this is all that leadership is.

Acknowledgements

This is the section of the book which you probably only read if you think you may be mentioned. Sorry – the chances are you're going to be disappointed. But you never know!

Throughout my career, every time I have applied for a promotion, my wife has expressed her support with the words 'but you're just a bozo'. I've always taken this as an attempt to keep me grounded, but in truth it is probably that she knows I do not possess any special talents. However, in the quarter of a century we have been together she has certainly noticed that I am unusually stubborn and determined. When I told her I was going to write a book, surprisingly, I was not mocked. I have drawn a great deal of confidence from this. So, firstly, I would like to say thank you to my wife, Victoria, without whom I would definitely be just another bozo.

Three complete strangers have encouraged me to write more, and I am grateful to them. Tom Rees took the direct approach in early 2019, telling me I should write a book, and offering some sage advice (following the publication of his excellent book, *Wholesome Leadership*, which I highly recommend). One instructive telephone conversation later and I had determined to fulfil a lifelong ambition. Tom and I hit it off – although I get the impression that Tom hits it off with most people he meets – and we have stayed in touch. He has been a great source of support and encouragement, and I am truly grateful to him.

Equally kind and brilliant, Christine Counsell and Dr Rebecca Allen read my blog from early on and have encouraged others to do so too.

When eloquent and intelligent people, such as Christine and Becky, praise your work, it is tremendously affirming. There are many others on Twitter who have liked, retweeted and posted positive reviews on my ramblings. Thank you, one and all.

A well-earned thank you goes to my erudite colleague, Emma White, who kindly proofread my work. There are few people in the world whom I would trust to read my first draft. Emma's knowledge of language and grammar is far superior to mine, and she tells it as it is – qualities I admire. Any mistakes which remain are mine, and all credit for readability goes to Emma.

If you have read this far without a mention, here is your chance. My final thanks go to all of you whom I have worked alongside since I started my teacher training in 1993. I have known so many talented teachers, inspiring leaders and incredible support staff. One of the messages of this book is that we should trust people to do their jobs. You are the experts – don't let anyone tell you otherwise!